Amberlie Johnson is a caring and outgoing person, whose life was turned upside down after she shut her eyes to go to sleep on an average, normal night. She enjoys working in the medical field, but her most joy in life is still having that one true love by her side. She never thought at 27f she would be getting her husband's affairs in order or hearing "code blue" all night, but this reminds her that life is too short and really living life to the fullest with those people you love!

We would love to dedicate this book to all the families who have lost or caring for someone with opiate addiction. We also want to dedicate this book to the survivors of opiate addiction and staying sober with this everyday battle.

Amberlie Johnson

ADDICTION: FROM THE OTHER SIDE

AUSTIN MACAULEY PUBLISHERS™
LONDON · CAMBRIDGE · NEW YORK · SHARJAH

Copyright © Amberlie Johnson 2023

All rights reserved. No part of this publication may be reproduced, distributed, or transmitted in any form or by any means, including photocopying, recording, or other electronic or mechanical methods, without the prior written permission of the publisher, except in the case of brief quotations embodied in critical reviews and certain other non-commercial uses permitted by copyright law. For permission requests, write to the publisher.

Any person who commits any unauthorized act in relation to this publication may be liable to criminal prosecution and civil claims for damages.

The story, the experiences, and the words are the author's alone.

Ordering Information
Quantity sales: Special discounts are available on quantity purchases by corporations, associations, and others. For details, contact the publisher at the address below.

Publisher's Cataloging-in-Publication data
Johnson, Amberlie
Addiction: From the Other Side

ISBN 9781649795274 (Paperback)
ISBN 9781649795281 (ePub e-book)

Library of Congress Control Number: 2023900576

www.austinmacauley.com/us

First Published 2023
Austin Macauley Publishers LLC
40 Wall Street, 33rd Floor, Suite 3302
New York, NY 10005
USA

mail-usa@austinmacauley.com
+1 (646) 5125767

I would love to thank my wonderful friends and family for sharing some hard but amazing stories of their battles with addiction. My biggest thank you is to my husband of the years and sharing his story and allowing the real truth behind this awful addiction and wanting to help people survive and encourage the way out.

Table of Contents

Chapter 1 — 11
My Story

Chapter 2 — 38
Why?

Chapter 3 — 50
Is It a Disease?

Chapter 4 — 58
Signs of Addict

Chapter 5 — 73
You're Not Alone

Chapter 6 — 83
The World Around You and Real-Life Stories

Chapter 7 — 90
What's the Next Step?

Chapter 1
My Story

As all stories are told with a beginning, middle and end. Well, mine had an end. Imagine having a wonderful life for 12 years, thoughts of a new house, maybe a baby, vacations, etc. You start your night off like any other, good dinner, great movie and then you fall asleep, all as normal. You then wake up to what you think is your dog having her cough episode, so you roll over to rub her belly and feel she is not next to you like she usually is, and see she is down by your feet and she has never done that and then you look over to find the one thing that would change your life forever.

You wake up to find your husband, the person you love, laying there with their head tilted back and halfway off the bed gasping for air and by the time you have grabbed your phone to call 911 and turn on the lights to see what happened, you watch all the life flush right out of him. Everything is white, from the lips to the pupils. You're frantic, you're trying to listen to the 911 caller and do what they are saying, and not sure what is happening so you smack him a few times and scream in his face thinking he's just sleep walking again or he's deep sleeping, no he died! All his bodily fluids exited his body. And just for a moment,

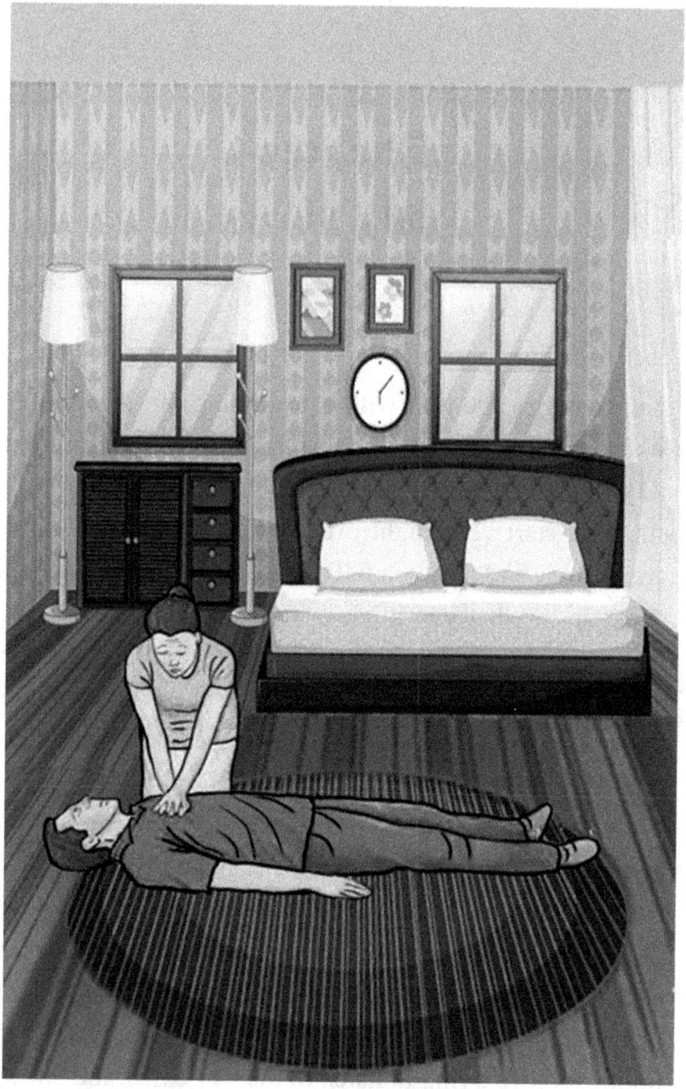

he was gone, this person I loved and cared for and planned to spend the rest of my life with. Then in minutes which seemed like hours, he flushed back all his color and started to grasp for air again. You get him on the floor finally to help his airway and still ask yourself what is happening, a seizure or a stroke? During this time, I had to figure out what to do with our two Pitbulls because they are very protective of us and especially, their daddy. So, you have to leave him, you have to follow the 911 callers instructions and get the dogs in another room and to do that, I had to get them downstairs behind the gate, and I don't know if they knew something was wrong, but this was the first time they came down the stairs without a fight and got right in the room so, I could put up the gate. I was thinking thank you God and please continue to help me through this night. Then the paramedics arrive and the first thing they ask you is, "What he is on?" And they keep asking and asking and you can only respond I don't know! Let's face it, you don't know, how could you and you think what are they talking about? What is he on? Then you have not only the paramedics, but the fire chief with the police chief trying to get your name and your birthday and you're nervous because you are thinking, are they going to try to trace whatever back to me or are they just doing their jobs? Even though a lot was going on, I was still able to give the correct information, which was a good thing, but still the feeling of all being lost and if they will be able to help him this time is all running through my head and will he survive this? As they work on the person you love, and he's struggling and fighting the EMTs to a point they had to literally, all seven of them, hold him down to just get the needle in for fluids

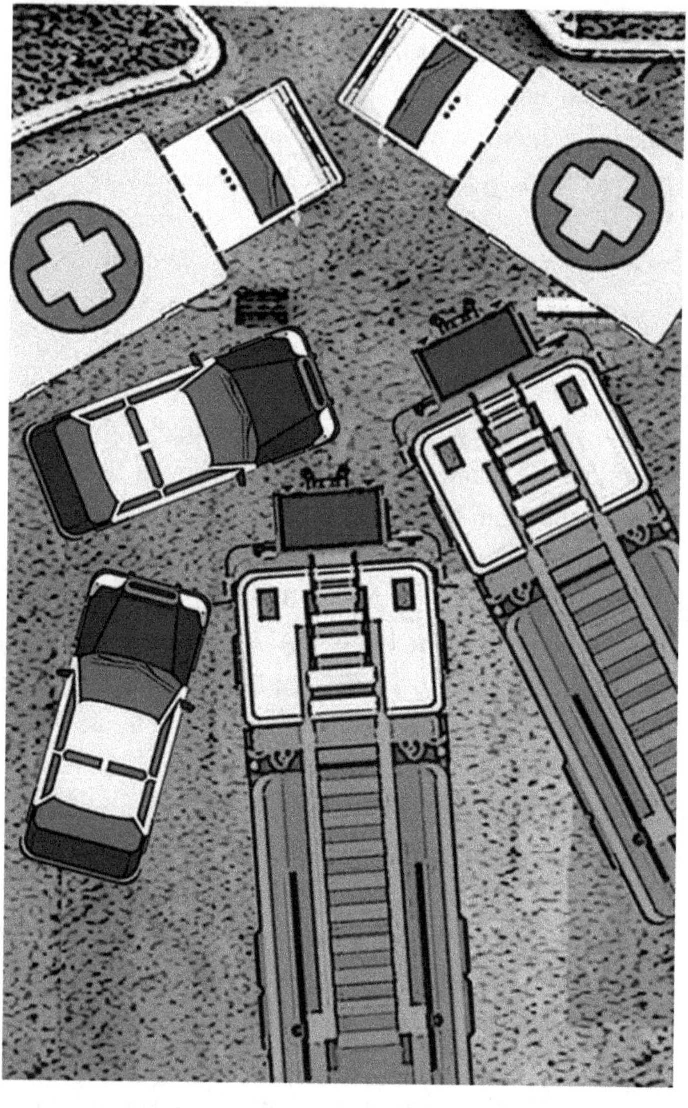

in his hand, and he still wasn't cooperating and I kept yelling to him as the police are trying to ask me questions, "Honey, it's going to be OK, please listen to them and just relax." Of course, they wouldn't let me back in the bedroom and I think if he was able to just see my face, he would have calmed down. He has always been like that, even with his previous hospital visit, if he can just see me and know I am there, regardless of the situation, he is at ease. Then I was trying to make out what he was saying and nothing coming out of his mouth makes sense like a stroke, your thinking, is this it? Finally, they were able to get the needle in his hand and were able to stand him up, because let's face it, we were on the top floor of the house and he's 6'8 and with all the curves and stairs, there was no way to get a board upstairs to take him down. When I finally see him stand up, I start to breathe again, a nice deep breath of relief, and I start to think it's OK, he's up, he's alert somewhat but, at least I can see his eyes and color in his face, but he still wasn't making sense and now it seems like he's not making sense like a drunk does when he has had too much to drink, so again I feel like maybe it will be OK. It takes thee seven EMTs to get him downstairs, three in front and four in the back, slowly making their way down, but he was able to stand up, which made me feel better. Then, they walk him out to a gurney outside get him to sit down on it, and strap him up. I remember him looking at me from the lawn on the gurney, and just could see the sadness in his eyes and how scared he was, so terrified like that maybe the last time he will look into my eyes. I just remember holding that door open and watching them strap him in and start to move him to the ambulance, to take him to the hospital. They close the ambulance doors and there are still two fire trucks, two police cars, and two ambulances outside your door in your street, and they are still talking in the lawn as they all exit my house. They had opened my screen door to lock it and then when asking them to help me unlock it they didn't know how, that did upset me because I had to go, I wanted to get right behind the ambulance when they would start to leave. You wonder why the ambulance is still, why aren't they moving? Only later do you find out that your husband died again and the paramedics had to shoot him up with Naloxone, a drug to treat a narcotic overdose in emergency situations like this one, and they kept telling him, "You're too young to die, stay with us!"

You're still in shock though, not sure what's happening and what to do next? You call all the people you can think of, in my case, I first called my mom, and I don't know why I did that since she is not in the area anymore, but I would always call her, she is my strong backbone and makes me feel like everything is going to be OK. She doesn't answer so I leave her a message. Then I think, who next? I call my boss because it's now 5 am and I know I am not going to work, but since he's a doctor and my boss, I text him, and immediately he calls me back right away, and says, "What happened, tell me everything that happened?" I began to explain and before I could go into more details, he said to me, "He's overdosed, please call me or have the hospital call me if there is anything I can do." I work for an amazing heart doctor who needless to say doesn't judge and supports me and helps not only me but anyone he can. I then reach out to his dad, who happens to be on the one vacation they would take all year, and leave him a message. By then, it's been like ten minutes, which seems like an hour. I hurry up, let the dogs out, while I get changed, grab just what I can, and get myself in the car. As I am driving, I start praying to God, "Please don't let him leave me, please save him. If all I can ask and pray for is you keep this giant man in my life and don't take him from me." I am literally making every light and if it was red, well sorry policeman, my husband could be dying and I am not going to just wait for a stupid red light. I finally got to the hospital and now it's about 5:30 am, and when I go to check-in, they just got him into a room, I rush in to see him, and his eyes are open, he's breathing, and looks just tired. I kept giving him kisses and just holding his hand, which seemed so cold, even with the warm blankets on him. I was just thanking God and crying in his arms while he kept yawning and shaking from what had happened. I got to meet the man nurse for the first time, and gosh if I could remember his name, but he really was the best nurse I have ever met, he took care of my husband the whole time in the ER that day. I finally get to speak with the doctor, the internist, and he is not telling me much but asks me to leave and speak with my husband by himself. I then use the opportunity to call my dad and let him know what's going on as much as I do, and of course, my dad's always trying to be supportive and encouraging and then making jokes to just try to cheer me up and it works for a minute or two and then the doctor comes out to speak with me and asks me to join the conversation in the room. As I come in, my husband has big eyes, like he does when he knows something and doesn't want to tell it, and then the doctor asks him again, this time in front of me, "We are treating you for an overdose and we need to know what you took this evening to cause this?" What, an overdose, I am thinking what the hell, his back on drugs again, this is an overdose, what the hell, what the fuck, what the everything. All I wanted to do at that moment was yell and curse him out till I was blue in the face, but instead, I waited to hear his reply. He looks at me and then back at the doctor and says, "I took nine Vicodin." The doctor says, "Is that all? Because this kind of overdose wouldn't be caused by that, and considering your long history with pills, this wouldn't just make your heart stop?" and my husband kept saying, "That's all I took." The doctor leaves and says, "You need to be honest with us or we can't help you." I look at him and tell him the same thing, "I don't care what you do or how much, you need to tell them so they can help you." Well, like an addict, he stuck to his story and wasn't budging from it.

I stepped out again to make one more call, and at this point, it's about 6:30 am now, I reached out to his grandma on his dad's side, she is my pal and I can count on and tell her anything, but the last thing I wanted to do was call her about her favorite grandson and he is in the hospital for an overdose and died already, but is doing fine now, but I had too. His family had to know, and it was my decision to do so, I mean I already called his dad, but someone in town had to know and help me. At this point in his life, he was very estranged from his mother, all she was doing was making him unhappy at this time and he just didn't want her to be a part of what was going on and I knew that, so I didn't call her at all, later I made the decision to go against his wishes because then there were no options left.

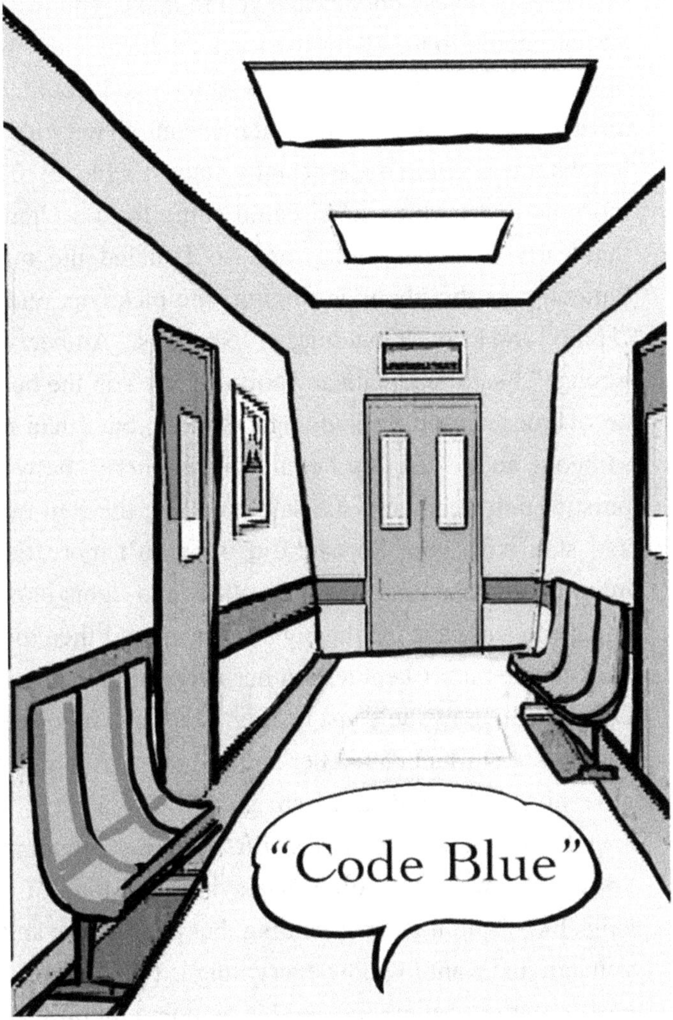
"Code Blue"

One of the worst things, from this whole day, is making phone calls. These phone calls you to make, you just know you are going to turn their lives upside down and it will be never-ending. When calling his grandma, I could barely have a gulp of spit to swallow, it made me so nervous to tell her what was going on, especially since it's like 6:30 in the morning and nothing good could come from a phone call that early in the morning, and so I dialed the number. Patiently, as the phone is ringing, she picks up, and says, "Hello" and I say, "Grandma, …" She says, "Amber, what's wrong?" I said just plain and simple, "He's in the hospital, he overdosed, and he is doing OK now, but I had to call someone and…" Before I could say anymore, she was just bursting into tears and she said I will be there in minutes and stay with you. So, she did. It wasn't more than 20 minutes, and she must have run all the red lights like I did, and came and gave me the biggest hug ever. I then took her back to see him. I kept telling her everything is good, he's OK for right now, he's just resting. She came in to see him, and he knew I had called her and to be ready, and she just gave him a kiss and said I am glad you're alive. I would spend the whole day in the ER with his grandma, not knowing if we were going or staying, and tons of phone calls, like I said it is never-ending, but people care and love you and just want to know everything is OK so you kind of just go with it. I think me and his grandma literally ate just one time that whole day and I think I went home to shower and feed the dogs and went through McDonald's drive-thru just to get us a burger. As the day went on, he was actually getting better, we were still in the ER, waiting to get a room

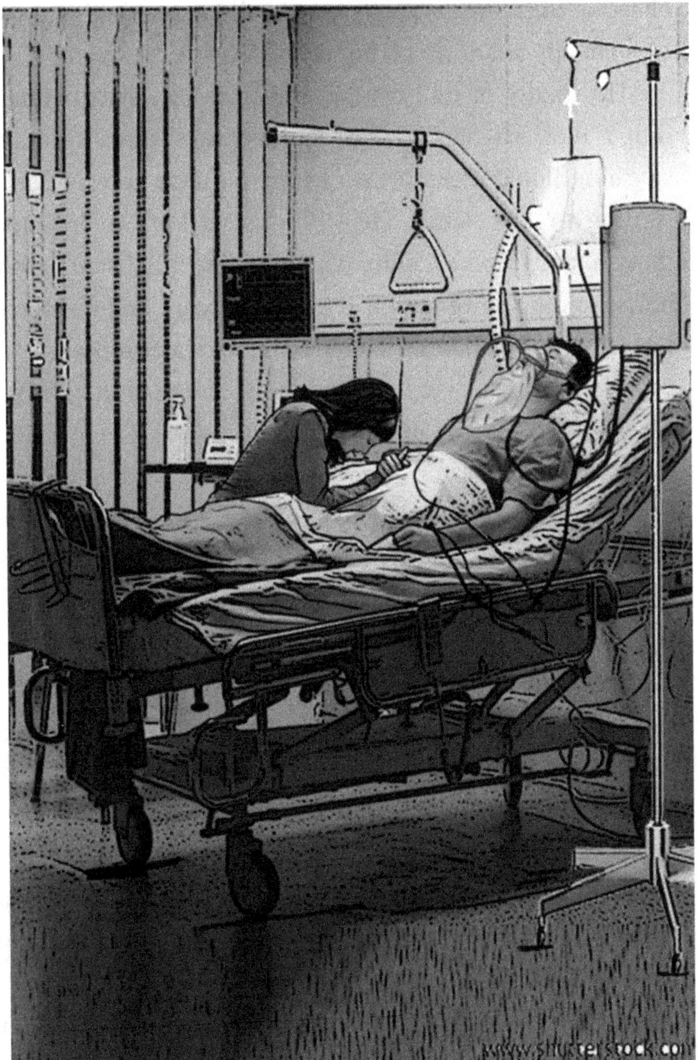
www.shutterstock.com

upstairs because they were going to just admit him for observation, which is protocol, and all I kept thinking, I will be so happy when we go home and was I ever wrong.

He finally is told by the nurse, he can start eating a liquid diet, so he can eat sherbert and some broth or anything liquid diet. He was happy because he was finally starting to feel better. He still was sticking to his story though, only nine Vicodin, which I knew like I said before, he is holding information back, he's lying and sooner or later the truth will have to come out, and later it does.

It's starting to get like 5 pm now, and then they finally have a room for him upstairs and they move him to the 2nd floor which is just for observation and we were all excited especially him, he's so tall he just doesn't fit in the ER beds. As we finally get him to that floor and in the room, as soon as they put the bed on breaks, all of sudden you hear Code Blue, Code Blue, and blue lights flashing, and you get nervous and then find out it's your loved one room they are rushing into, he had coded. He had turned over and looked like he was getting comfortable to go back to sleep and he just flatlined. I had never seen so many people rush into one room before in my life, and it had to have been like 15 people. I remember looking in and just being in shock, what the hell is wrong with him, why is he OK one minute not even that all day and then going back into coding again? I look and see a guy on his chest giving him compressions and then they say, "Hold" and they shock him, then they say he's back. The new internist on that floor comes out, and I swear was an idiot, says he's fine and we are not sure why this happened and we are going to move him to ICU. Which in my professional opinion should have been the first place they should have put him since no one knew really what he was coming off of and what would really happen next. They finally get him stable to move and we move him up to the ICU Floor for a lot of you who don't know it's the intensive care unit floor. It goes on 8 pm and everything has been silent and still, he was alert and doing better, so I left to go to my dad's to get a charger because he was like two blocks from the hospital, in case I needed to get back, and of course as soon as I pulled up and go in the house to tell my dad what was going on and grab the charger, no later did I get a call he was coding again. I raced as fast as I could to get back to the hospital, and I run-up to the hospital doors to find they are locked, and then I see a security guard and yelling at him I say it's my husband that is coding please let me in, thank god he did, and I finally go up to the ICU Floor and his grandma is screaming they are trying to work on him and she is yelling in my ear his name and all I can do is just be stunned in disbelief this is really happening, he could really die on me. Then you know it's bad when you see the priest coming down the hallway because he heard code blue and I thought please don't come to talk to me because this isn't it, he will make it.

He makes it back to me again, he comes back now the fourth time, and I remember the head nurse coming down to me and saying we really need to know what he is on and I still couldn't give them any answers, God, he wasn't even being honest with me and why are you talking to me right now, he could die and you want to talk about this now. When he is finally stable again, I told the internist you need to call a cardiologist, it's obviously his heart and it just won't stand this anymore, and the internist is constantly

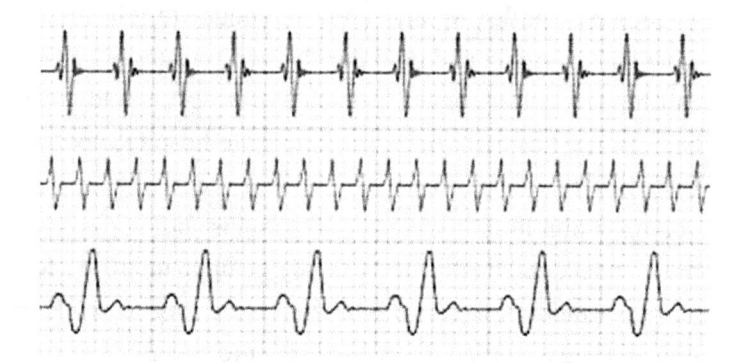

arguing with me and saying he will when he thinks it's necessary and I said it's necessary and to call my doctor I work for, and then he starts to argue with me more and says it will have to be an on-call physician and I said well I am on the phone with him right now and he says he will come in right now if you put in the consult. I can see why all our patients have a hard time getting my doctor to come to see them, because it literally took my husband four times, yea four times, for his heart to stop before this hospital saw it necessary to call a cardiologist. Let's define the word cardiologist-specialist for the heart when your heart keeps stopping. What idiots!

I finally am able to go by my husband's bedside and now it's about 9 pm and his grandma is there with me, and I hold his hand, and say, it's time to call your mother and tell her what is going on. He keeps saying no and I finally made the decision to call her. Wow, was that ever a mistake I made, you know you make the right decision because you're a good person and no matter what has happened, I didn't know if he was going to live past the night and I didn't want his mom to never know, so I made the call and as soon as she answers, I say, "Hey, he's in the hospital, he overdosed and he has coded a couple of times, and I made the decision to call you and we need you to come to the hospital now." All she is doing is crying and I can tell she had been drinking a lot I was worried about her even coming up in the hospital but I had to, and I know even now I made the right decision even though it later blows up in my face.

I go back in and tell him his mom will be here shortly, and finally, she comes with his other grandma, and O Boy, does the shit hit the fan. She comes in smelling like alcohol and smoke, I mean just terrible, and says, "Why the fuck am I just getting told now he is in the hospital and why the Fuck only now?" and I said, "Because he didn't even want me to call you and I did because I thought you should know and be here because I didn't think he was going to make it so, I went against his wishes." And she said OK that's understandable and then when she tried to say more, his grandma on his dads side said, "Don't you fucking even start right now, don't you say shit in this room, don't you fucking start shit." So we all exited the room and his dad was calling, I remember at this time, and as I was talking to him, Code Blue happened again. And this time, I was down on my knees praying for forgiveness of all my sins and everyone's sins and praying if you get him out of this I will do anything and everything and whatever you ask of me. My husband was literally gone for almost four minutes, four minutes of complete silence and chills and shakes and tears and is this the end, he's really going to leave me for good, not just to go away but go away forever. Then all these thoughts are running through your head as people are screaming and crying and yelling, as if time stops itself, and you think God Dammit why was I so stupid, why could of just been stronger, been more alert, he's a great person and I was such a dumb ass leaving it all up to him to be strong and say no and his dying look he's dying and there is nothing I can do anymore. He is just going to be a body in the ground and it's all my fault. And then, the Code Blue Stops, you don't know if he died or what happened it's just complete silence and then you see the priest again and fear for the worst. Could his body really withstand all these breakdowns and could his body come back and function with all the shut downs?

As the next 24 hours go, my husband died five times all together that day and the last one I didn't think he was coming back. Days turned into nights and nights turned into days. I thought the first 24 hours was bad, well that was only the beginning.

Finally, the doctor I work for made his way to the hospital and into my husband's room and the curtains were drawn, was it because he died and they were making a confirmation, or was he alive? A matter of minutes seemed hours and all I could do was wait in the worst hallway of the hospital to see if the last thing I said to my husband was, "Tell the truth, what drugs are you taking?" Not I love you or stay with me or don't leave me or my world will be empty without you, it was what drugs are you taking? Always remember to not end on a bad note because you never know when it will be the last time you talk to the person you love.

My doctor comes out and says, "We have him stabilized and if he would have been out any longer, he would have had brain damage." I just got down on my knees and prayed for every kind of forgiveness and thanks to the all mighty God. Luck can only take you so far, but what they told me next, luck had nothing to do with it. The head nurse then told me, they are running labs, but as it looks, his heart seems to be the only thing to be affected at this time. I am praying even more to the almighty because to not have failing organs after all the time his heart stopped and he was gone, he wasn't lucky, he was blessed by the big man upstairs looking down on him.

I thought from this point on, we are in recovery and I can finally go home and sleep and feel at ease, boy was I wrong.

It's now been 36 hours, about a few dozen phone calls later telling everyone he has survived and is stable, nothing to eat and no sleep, and haven't even made it home again, which luckily I have an amazing brother who helped me out after all this and took care of my house and dogs. I felt I needed to stay with him, I am his wife, that night, I felt like I couldn't leave him because I don't know if this new combination of bags of fluid IV in him will keep him alive, so I stayed that night. He had a nurse in the room with him 24 hours starting that evening, at all times, and she was amazing. I don't think people really realize, but the nurses are what keep a person alive in a hospital setting, especially that floor. Even though I think my husband felt guilty about a lot of things and was just unsure even what all happened, this nurse would make him laugh and keep him alive the best she could. Unfortunately, the medications were keeping him from going back to episodes of coding but through the night, he was going back into those arrhythmias in his EKGs that were almost back to him dying once again. He actually could start feeling when he was, and of course, even when I thought I would be able to sleep, it just wasn't an option.

Now we come to 48 hours, still, no sleep and no shower, which I don't shower, but I just couldn't leave his side thinking if something happens I'm so far away which also kept me from working and luckily, I had an amazing heart doctor as well as my boss watching over my husband so the situation was understood, but couldn't keep my life on hold forever. His grandma came back that day and even though everything was looking better, his dad still took an earlier flight to cut his vacation short to be with his son. His grandma and I became even more amazing friends through this whole situation. She looked at me and said, "Go home and at least shower, he will be fine."

I looked at my husband and said, "If I leave, nothing better happens while I am gone."

He said to me that day, "I will be here waiting for you when you get back." So, I finally got to go home for the first time in two days and be with my dogs and cry because I didn't want to cry in front of him and it's all the no sleep and exhaustion from everything but I was able to shower and relax for a little bit and then back to the hospital I went. Luckily, I have an amazing best friend, who happens to be a lawyer, and came to the hospital that day. She said you're crazy to not get POA paperwork in order, just in case and boy was she ever right. It's the type of thing you never think about because it's like why to think about dying at thirty, but you should, especially if you have someone who does drugs or has a drug history or just anyone in general. Death can happen anytime and any day and one should always live life to the fullest. She told him later after she visited him in the hospital, she said she couldn't even find her car in the parking lot, because the way he looked and seeing him like that, just made her cry and be lost. It took her over an hour to find her car. My bestie and my husband have been friends since they were kids like kindergarten kids.

Her house was right behind his grandma's house and since he was always there, they always hung out, until one day, when everyone started getting older, her mom said,

"You know, He can't spend the night anymore." Of course, we laugh about it now, but they could never understand why then. Memories like that were flushing out the next day when I talked to her because my husband has always been her best bud as well and you just never want to see someone like that ever in your whole life.

The whole day goes on by and he does great. His vitals stayed within normal and he was back to eating a liquid diet because at this point, he was not allowed even water, but his heart doctor OK'd him to start a liquid diet, which is not much, but it was something. So, the day was going really well. Even his mother stopped back in and luckily hadn't been drinking or smoking which was good because my husband said he did not want that around him because it made him just nauseous. I have never really liked his mom for a long time and being in the same area was hard enough to swallow, and it would be even harder to come to truths due to the nature of what was coming next, but she was being civil and I still had my guard as usual. I let him visit with her and he was happy I made the decision I did to call her and I think it had a lot to do with shame and embarrassment on his part and didn't want them, "I told you," and this and that usually comes from a situation like this, but she actually just was happy he was alive and doing better. His grandma and I talked about it and agreed she would stay with him the next night now we are going on day three and I said that's fine and she would call me if anything happened. Well, my husband was fine with it too and said he would just be fine. So I left later in the evening about 8 pm and went home to just sleep in my own bed. I think it was about 3 am, if I remember correctly, which I was so exhausted at that point I literally touched that pillow with my head and I was out cold. I remember his grandma saying he keeps going into those pre episodes prior to his coding and I needed to get to the hospital. So I quickly just went with what I was wearing earlier that evening and grabbed my purse and I was off again. When finally getting up to his room, he was going in and out of them but then became stable again. Like I said, I thought my nightmare was over and it was OK to leave him alone and then I just couldn't leave him again. By this time, his grandma as well as I have not gotten sleep in almost 72 hours and it's going on day four now. The doctors really had been harassing my husband to be completely honest on what drugs he had been taking that day and finally, my doctor was just over it and said I need everyone to leave the room. As we left, I saw the look in his eyes, and that's the I mean business look and I don't even mess with that look so I was hoping he would finally be honest with someone, well he was. My doctor said to come back in and that my husband had something to tell me and as I entered the room, I could see the scared look of a little child on his face and he was just terrified that he had to admit not only but tell me to my face. He says with tears in his eyes and breathing heavily, "I need to tell you the truth now, it depends on my life and care, I did heroin and I have been doing heroin and that's why I am here." It was almost a sign of relief and I wasn't even mad surprisingly, I was just happy he finally told the truth. I guess that's what it is with addicts, something so good and so great in your life, and then finally when your life is gone, you want to take a leap of redemption? That's funny, yea right, he would have kept lying his whole way to death which he pretty much did, but my doctor said he wouldn't take care of him anymore or get the right doctors to help him and he would just die. He finally made the right decision and wanted help and he got it. My doctor refers him to another cardiologist, a personal friend, due to the fact I do work for the man and it is in somewhat conflict of interest in the health field so, with that understanding, we wait and see how my husband does for the rest of the day and if he can remain stable off the IV drugs then, he will not need to have any surgery. Later on that day, he has an ultrasound of his heart which shows a normal ejection fraction which means it's normal and the EKG tracings of his heart are doing well and he was moved up on the liquid diet to the next level which now he could have oatmeal and other things, not just broth and water and ice melts. Everything was looking up and the thought of him not having to have surgery was out the window.

Later that day, his dad arrived and was just so happy to see his son alive and alert. He looked at me and his mom and said, "You both need to go home and rest and I want to stay with my son and have some long talks with him." At this point, with the doctors really knowing what they are finally treating him for and the knowing of the good doctors and right care in place, I felt like I could leave him again. We both took his dad's advice and kissed him goodbye at about seven that evening and left. That night was the first night in five days I could finally rest.

When I got to the hospital the next day, my doctor called me and said he spoke with his personal friend, my husband's new cardiologist all night and they both came to the conclusion if my husband cannot support his heart off the IV Drugs then he will need to have a device implant, in his heart, to help keep it in rhythm and shock him if he would ever go back into those arrhythmias again to save his life. This device would help pace his heart to a normal heart rate, not 35 where he was and had been, and shock him, like paddles to his chest, if he went out of rhythm which he was continually doing when trying to wean off the IVs. So I knew then, he was going to have to have this device implanted and have major heart surgery and he may not make it through that. As I tell my story, and your reading this, I hope you relay this information to the person you know in your life that is an addict, because it never gets easier, even when I thought I had saved his life, there was still another obstacle he had to go through to maybe still live his life again.

That morning, the new cardiologist came in and I knew him, and he looked at me and my husband and the rest of the family there, his mom, dad, and grandma, and said he will have this device and there is no other option. He spoke with my husband privately, and he agreed. He had to go on NPO, with nothing to eat or drink, at that moment because they would do surgery that afternoon. I was a nervous wreck the whole day. I couldn't eat or focus or anything. I couldn't talk anymore or laugh or pick up my phone. I did make one call and that was to my brother because I needed him there, someone from my family, to just be there to help me go through it. His surgery took a whole three hours and normally this surgery takes two hours, and even knowing he was in the best hands in this area, and nothing could go wrong, I still cried and worried and picked at myself and just kept pacing, I couldn't imagine losing him all over again and not being able to save him. You then start to think about all the stupid fights and stupid things you say to that person, which you always regret later, but you think about those times and geez those could have been your last words and if he makes it out of this, I will try my best to always say I love you and give him a kiss and just hold him. Just please God make him come out of this alive and well. That was the scariest time of my life and I hope the only scary time in my life because I know deep down, I won't do this again and I will never go through another time like this again ever.

My husband, 32 years old, went through the first major surgery of his life and survived, with a pacemaker defibrillator keeping him alive to pace his heart at a normal rate and a defibrillator to shock him literally like paddles on your chest to bring him back. He has the heart of a 70-year-old now. He has prolonged QT syndrome which happens after an overdose and prolonged use of drugs like opiates and heroin. He will never be the same man I started to date right out of high school or be able to do everything he wants to now. We don't even know if he will live a full life. That's what addiction is. Life alternates and eventually death.

Well like I said there is always a beginning to a story and ours was actually a pretty fun and crazy one! Relationships all start out like Candy Canes and Lollipops. All the good things in life blossom with a new love.

My husband and I were friends actually before we became a couple which most people are and I remember our fun and crazy night in Fort Wayne with all of our friends on the way back, I had to sit in the back seat, and since he's like 6'8 he had to sit in the front seat, and he held his hand behind his seat the whole way home, which was like two hours, just to hold my hand the whole way. When we got home, he helped carry my bags in and kissed me on the cheek, and said I will call you later. I thought yea, sure, that's what they all say right? Well later on in the evening, he did call and so I picked up and said, "What's up?" And he says, "Well just wanted to see if you wanted to come over and watch movies and stuff?" And just the way he said it, I couldn't say no. Right there, is how it all began, I don't have to go through all that but my husband was a fun and loving and caring person who loved to just do about everything and ate just about everything too, even those awful homemade mash potatoes I made for the first time, just awful! We used to play video games, cook out, go on vacations, etc. We even bought our first house 10 years ago and got married five years ago. Somewhere in our story, I lost him. I lost the caring, truthful, loveable person I've stuck by and even married. I am faced now and for many years a person who only says I love you because you do, doesn't do anything or want to do anything like play video games or go on vacations, begins to lie all the time, starts stealing stuff from our house and from other people, cleans out your bank accounts so all the money you have worked hard every week is gone, and just sits in a chair and says nothing. You will read throughout this book how an amazing person can go from this to the end and how I hope this book will encourage and give strength to you more than I ever had and try to save that person's life and your own!

You need to remember you! Be strong and willing to make the right decision! Life sucks and no one says anything about ever being easy. Whether it's your father or mother, husband or wife, brother or sister, child, or even your best friend, sometimes you have to stop being the enabler and cut ties! Hold your ground! You're stronger than you think you are! Believe me, after 12 years, I finally have done it! Hold my own and believe in myself! Whatever you decide, whether to keep that person in your life or dismiss them, like one of my friends said, "So who cares if you love an addict, do you!" Just remember to not enable them! The main goal is sobriety and saving their life because deep down you love and care for them but you can only do so much! Treatment and sobriety are in the eye of the beholder and they have to do it for them and no one else!

" Sobriety is worth it",
"Love and Cherish Everyday",
"Don't Enable Them",
"Choose Life"

Chapter 2
Why?

Why? I have asked myself this question over and over again. It's almost like asking yourself, "Who, what, and where?" and never really coming to a conclusion or the right answer. You wonder why a person who loves you and you love them back can do something to only hurt you and the others around them. You sit and wonder is it me? Did I make them do this? What is wrong with me? So many questions run through the mind of a person on the other side of someone dealing with addiction of any sort. My story and this book revolve around the epidemic we are faced with opiate addiction. I have been a victim of this for over 12 years, but a lot of those years I didn't even know. Someone who is addicted to something whether it be pills or any type of drug has a great way of hiding it. Why you ask, well the obvious answer is they don't want to get caught. They like the feeling and want to try to keep everything in their life as it is and not lose one thing. They manage to hide it not only from their spouse or relationship there, but those around them, like family, friends, coworkers, etc.

Let's face reality here, you will never know really why a person starts drugs or why they continue to take them. It's a way of life for them. They can be in a place where they can hold back feelings, emotions, and no fears. You then start to ask yourself or people have asked me, why do you deal with this person? Or why do you stay with this person? I turn and simply say because I love him. It's harder than you think to say goodbye to someone you love and spend all the time you have in this world with them and just throw it out the window. It's hard to watch that person you love just throw their life away when they have so much potential to do something with their life.

Why is this an epidemic? It finally comes clear to a person looking on the outside, when you are faced with commercials and now even the news is constantly making it a known issue. Which is great. I mean let's bypass the fact we think as a society that marijuana is the worst drug out there and for a long time that's all we heard. I am going, to be honest, at one point I tried it, and I think everyone has at one point in their lives. Actually, when I meant my husband that was something we were doing together when it used to be fun to have a few drinks and smoke some marijuana and play old school videos and just kick it, but as you watch and read now, the heat is off marijuana and now onto an opiate epidemic. When reading articles, they point out it's the worst drug crisis in American History. Then you think to yourself, wow and they were worried about marijuana all this time. It's even been made a statement in lots of articles that there are more than twice as many motor vehicle deaths as fatal drug overdoses.

The problem we are faced with starts out as a simple gesture of taking a pill. Usually, it starts out with some doctor prescribing it for whatever reason or a family member or friend giving you a pill of some sort to say, "You will feel better with this and it's OK to have one with your beer." However it starts, it starts, and the epidemic and your life's on the line. Now, a lot of people say it starts with doing drugs like marijuana or drinking at an early age, I personally think it has nothing to do with that. Not only as adults but as parents with your children, you need to be on the lookout for this to be at your doorstep.

OK parents, wake up, this epidemic is for you too. You are the ones with the medication scripts that can lead to these new party ideas now. Lock it up! Keep an eye out! I know there is only so much you can do but hey, I used to hate my mom for telling me I couldn't go out or hang out with this person or come home by nine, well guess what, it worked! I am thankful and blessed to have had a mean parent because with that guidance I chose and still do the right thing! I mean we all do stupid things, even the huge party I threw at my dad's in high school, but as parents, as I see now and didn't then, the harsh reality is to be strict and have them not like your decisions. Back then, it was drinking and maybe smoking marijuana but now that's lame and kids are finding the new way. We all had D.A.R.E. education, right, but it sinks in for only that period of time. It's time to stand up and do your part too!

You have today with young people, teenagers, throwing these "Skittle Parties" or "Pharming Parties" which are parties everyone brings what pills they have or have access to and you mix it in a bowl. Then someone takes one of whatever and you see the high you get from it. So you end up going to a party with your friends and they say, "It will be fun, try this one." With these parties, like the saying goes,

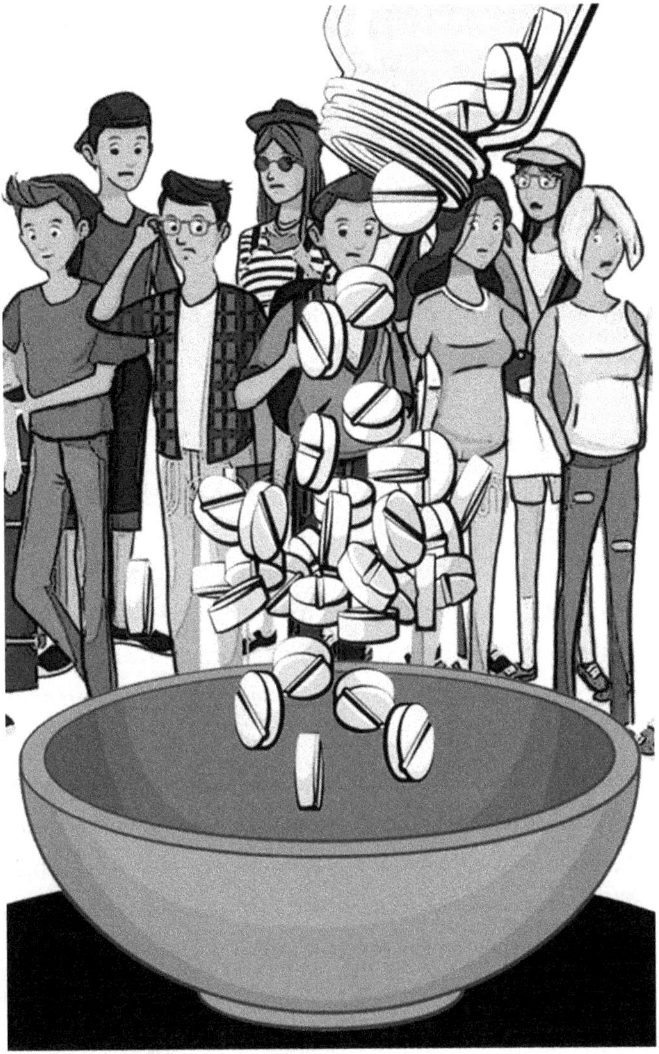

"Boys will be boys," well "kids will be kids" and they will go with whatever their friends are doing and finding prescription drugs is a lot easier to come by even for them because parents take them and are available in your homes. The one thing kids will never understand, just like adults, these drugs will eventually kill you and the epidemic of addiction is now starting at an earlier age, just like everything else to pregnancy and even drinking. The epidemic isn't just with adults, as most of the information we read and watch, but with our youth. I mean you don't have to worry about your kids drinking anymore, the new high is out there.

I've had not only teenagers I know now that have passed away from this opiate use but close friends of ours! Like one of my dad's friends, the father of our friends said, "We should never have to bury them, they should be burying us." Remember it only takes that one pill, that one time, that one party, and you're gone! Your body can only withstand so much before it shuts down completely and then there's no coming back! Did you know it only takes four minutes of being flat-lined to cause permanent brain damage? Your son or daughter would be a vegetable and there's nothing you can do, but you could have tried in the beginning. I know it's hard to even with my life and my husband, but what I deal with his parents shows me how hard it is even for them to say, "You have a problem and please get help." You never want to believe your kid is doing drugs, but again wake up! Be alert! Later on, I will go over signs I have seen over my period of time and maybe it will be an eye-opener to help or to just be aware! I never want another parent, husband or wife, or even grandparents to go through all that we have in our lives!

Even with our youth, I feel it starts with someone who is vulnerable and trusts the person giving them the drugs, whether it's the doctor or family member or friend, etc. My journey has been with all sides of this. Starting out, again I never knew this information and it took me years, I mean years, to finally see, and unfortunately as you will find out almost too late to do something. The worst can happen and I know it's hard to not be ashamed or be hesitant to come to someone and say, "I know you're using and please find help," but you have to be strong and stand up because one day it will kill that person and don't make the mistake I did and waited.

My husband started out with going to see a physician for back pain and the physician wrote him a 90 day supply, one tablet by mouth four times daily as needed, which is 360 tablets of Norco's, and said, "Take when needed." Well, that's how it all starts. At first, that's what my husband did and followed instructions, but the problem you run into is what do you do when you are out of pills? The first thought is well they seek and find, nope. What you do is find another doctor and go in and establish care to get them to write you a script. You then start getting letters that can't be seen anymore at different offices due to them finding out you have been jumping from doctor to doctor to get pills. In the end, you never can be seen by these doctors again or their facilities and let's face it, it's hard enough to find a doctor and if anyone that is reading this book that is an addict, know that you will need a doctor eventually and as I stand right now, it's impossible to find my husband one that will take him, so when you have to be on pills to actually keep you alive, think twice.

Unfortunately, for my husband, he started seeing a physician that was actually later on arrested for writing scripts of narcotics for no apparent diagnosis and will be in jail for a very long time. Not only for my husband but for anyone there that has dealt with this and they wonder why opiate addiction is an epidemic. You have physicians writing scripts like this one and for crazy amounts for a patient to have on hand and they wonder why people are dying from this. Come to my very question of why do doctors even write these kinds of drugs? Why can't they recommend something less strong and non-addicting to start a patient out? Eventually, doctors do run out, and it leads an addict to seek and find.

Recently, within this year, the idea of doctors prescribing addictive drugs like opiates has come to the surface and hospitals have been trying to raise awareness on what to do and what not to do with prescribing these types of drugs in meetings and seminars. Finally, a doctor stands up and says, "No, I will not prescribe you opiates"; unfortunately, later that day the doctor was shot point-blank and killed. This patient and her husband made a new patient appointment to see this bone specialist regarding some kind of pain and just like an addict would do is to search out and try to see multiple doctors for one time new patient visits to just getting their fix. Well, this patient was unhappy with the physician when he disagreed and said he would not write the prescription and try other things to help with the pain. Later on in the day, the husband came back to the office and waited till the physician walked out to his car and shot him point-blank, and killed him right in the parking lot. Not much later, after the lockdown with the facilities and hospital and countless searching and reviewing cameras and statements, the car of the husband was found not far from a friend's house of theirs and he was then found later in the yard of that house and had shot himself to death. What will doctors do now? Will they still stand up and try to help beat this epidemic or now, stand down due to recent events? Only time will tell, I'm afraid. As one person stated, "Now we are killing doctors." I know people are wondering why and what could be going through the mind of this guy and his wife, why would they kill the doctor who just simply said no and not just go and seek the drugs elsewhere? The world we live in now is scary and uncertain. The use of a gun seems a way to solve anything and apparently this was not a smart addict, because there are other ways to get drugs. You will never know what and why an addict does something, as I have said before, and this is just another reason to prove my point. The mind of an addict is an unknown mystery and unless we are ones ourselves, will we ever know the truth behind their thinking? They can tell us all they want, but to really know, we would have to become one and there is no sense in that either.

Life is a crazy and wild ride and just when you think you know what someone will do they come out and shock you again. My husband never had the urge, at least I don't think so, to go murder a physician for saying no, but again I don't think that ever happened to him either. I almost wish this patient's wife would have just sought out these drugs elsewhere or had an addict, which I am sure she is friends with, say hey I will give you some or hear go to this person.

Addicts always have friends that are doing the drugs with them, so you probably have been introduced to them at one point in your life. My husband would just introduce them as someone he worked with or just merely met and said, "Hey this is my friend so and so and I invited him to our party is that OK?" Of course, you're going to say it's OK or to a family gathering, of course, you are, because one, you're not thinking they are on drugs and two, you're a person who always says it's OK and they know that, trust me. Then you meet these new friends and you just know something is off but you're having fun yourself so you don't think much about it. Then he starts to mention these people's names more and that he's going to hang out with them or take your dog for a walk and O, I bumped into him while I was out, and then he stops bringing these people over and you realize they aren't coming around to family events or things your hosting and inviting them too. Something deep down in an addict says, "I better keep them away and not bring around them too much or they may catch on I am doing drugs."

Years ago, before I really started tailgating with his family, my husband brought a friend he called with him to this tailgate. This friend was someone I still never have met to this day but was skinny and lots of scabs and sores on his face and arms and was not wearing a shirt and just looked exactly like what a drug addict would look like, and my husband, of course, introduced him like hey this is my friend so and so and hey this is my family. No one would think anything of it, but when you have a family like mine or his, were not rich but were not poor either and the friends we do have would never look like that let alone ever be introduced to our families. Well, his dad knew something was up because my husband was looking odd and you have to remember this is when we didn't know and just thought like always. "He's been drinking or he's been getting high and smoking weed with his friends again." And of course, my husband would say, "We have been partying all day." What are you to think when yea, you can party all day and look like that, I do sometimes for sure. Even when, as a parent, what do you say? Of course, his dad went along with his story and said, "Hey I am so and so and you guys are more than welcome to eat and drink and have fun! It's game day!" His dad then told me they didn't long just a few minutes and had left. He always says, "I wish I would have known and would have said something." But, how do you know that? You don't. I can sit here and say the same thing, but I didn't do anything when he would bring friends like that around at our get-together or even when people would stop by the house. Wow, what can I tell you about that and how annoying that was, I mean people would drive by slow by the house, even though I know we don't live in the best neighborhood, still was weird, and then cars just pulling up or be parked in front when I got home and he wasn't even there, or how we would be sitting and watching something on TV and he would just randomly start to get up and say he had to go out to his work truck or the car to get something and then I would look out the window, finally after multiple times this was happening, to see someone just talking to him through their window and then them driving away and he comes back and I would say, "Who was that and what was that all about?" and he would simply say, without hesitation, "O nothing, just someone from work." It got to the point, I finally started going outside after him just to see what was going on, and then once someone in the car or he saw me, he would say Hey I will be right in or what Babe or the car would simply start to drive away. I mean I never knew what was really going on, but always knew it wasn't good, and that's what I mean about your gut feeling and reaction. Trust yourself and say something! At that time, instead, I would just back inside and not think anything of it, just thought hey they wanted to just stop by to say hey or maybe they were in the neighborhood. Addicts will try to keep everything within the normal and continue to change things up to keep you guessing as for instant people would just start coming to the house and not when I was there, and like a dumb person, I would always call my husband and tell him I was coming home or when I was and then he would know when and how long to have someone there. I knew they were coming into the house or he was meeting them because less and less were just pulling up to the house and when I would get home, I could tell people have been in my house, stuff moved or someone was sitting on the couch, even when he would deny it and say no one was here or simply say well, yea o yea so and so stopped by, when I knew he hasn't seen that guy in a long time. Deny, Deny, Deny, I swear that's all he would do from that point on, and then you just stop asking because it's Deny Deny Deny. Addicts do this because they love their new life and new friends and want every lie and dishonest things they have done kept secret and keep their lives in perfect harmony.

    Why does someone continue to kill themselves? Why do they expect forgiveness from everyone around them when they are the ones doing it to themselves and forgiveness should not be given?

Why do you seem like you're in a tunnel of darkness, a black hole, and you're so deep you can't even crawl out? You seem to find a way to reach the light but the black the hole of darkness seems to cradle you back in. What makes us think we can change someone all by ourselves? Is it the hope of once what was or the desire to keep the only thing we know? Life is unpredictable and the more we try to anticipate the outcome, the more we keep ourselves in the dark.

There are so many why questions, it's impossible to answer them all. Just always have an outlet whether it's a best friend or a family member, or even a therapist. You will need someone to help you get through this. As a friend of mine would say, "It's hard as fuck." It's too hard and too painful to do it on your own, trust me when I say this because I've been there and I am there and struggled through this addiction disease by myself and it never got me anywhere. It did get me a lot of lonely nights crying to sleep and wondering why I still live and deal with everything. Why, you ask, because you amazing, and life is too amazing to let everything go for someone who doesn't care about their life or your own.

Chapter 3
Is It a Disease?

IT IS A DISEASE
It's a disease of the mind. It affects a lot of things, not only how you act and talk, but your weight, appearance, body, and mind. You don't have a major weight loss but someone like my husband from 250 to 180 at the time of check-in at the hospital, affects your way of life. Your appearance, some can pull it off with you never even knowing but some not so lucky. Scabs and lots of irritated skin from constantly trying to pop that pimple or just think it is, to dark bags under the eyes because you're not really sleeping, it's like drunken sleep you don't really sleep. Even with appearance changes, you don't notice it because you're seeing it every day plus you don't even know their own drugs. Listen to your friends or family when they tell you because they are looking from the outside in and they see it faster than we will. It's almost like we are too comfortable and too busy to notice.

I think out of spite and anger you say Disease yea right? Really? How can something you can "say no" be a disease? Then you watch someone right in front of your eyes crying for help, and say, "What's wrong with me? I don't know what's wrong with me?" I think the diseased part of someone loves you, because when an addict says they love you, how can they love you without loving themselves? How can an addict care about someone if they don't care about themselves? That's when I think it's coming close to a disease, a disease that is ending their lives and they finally realize it.

Now you can't say it's a disease like cancer, but it is some form of disease. A disease is defined as well as a particular quality, habit, or disposition regarded as adversely affecting a person or group of people. Well, that's an addiction to a T. Unfortunately, there is no cure for this. People will always be an addict, the only hope is they find a way in their minds to beat it.

Just like any kind of disease or someone that is ill, you have to want to make the effort and help that person along their way to recovery.

Addicts are always in recovery. This disease keeps them fighting a battle some think they can never win. I have seen recovering addicts beat this addiction and be sober 5, 7, 10 years with no problem and you think they aren't battling anymore, Think again! It's a lifelong battle and if you're in a relationship with an addict, it's a lifelong battle for you too.

With addicts, it's what the next high is? Their bodies just like anybody else adapts to something and you just don't get the high you did before so you need to go to the next level. In their minds, it goes maybe Norco or Percocet to smoking or sniffing heroin or cocaine and then leads to injecting themselves with needles, which then leads to death. Some people only make it past the pills because not only do they swallow them but they can crush and snort them, so even if you find yourself with an addict who is just doing pills, how are they doing pills? I mean not only ingesting messes with your intestines and stomach and even your bowels! Really, how do you think my husband had his 1st hospital visit, bleeding from the ass, let's get real here. This shit is no joke! Now if you're snorting you're messing with your lungs and guess what, those can bleed too and kill you!

These drugs are like acid just burning through your body. Is it really worth it? Addicts think so because they only want to have their next high to forget about their problems and live in a carefree State of mind. Adult choices and real-life things scare any adult but especially a sober addict for the 1st time. They aren't able to hide behind the walls of a secure inpatient rehab clinic anymore.

This disease can affect anyone and even the people you think don't do drugs, like opiates, but yes, they do. It can be the school bus driver, the principal at your kids' school, the police chief, and even can be the priest at your church. It is true! People will surprise you, but they don't surprise me anymore. That's why it is so important to pay attention in this world anymore, it is the people you never suspect. It is like a nice married couple living in your neighborhood, maybe even next door to you, and guess what? They are probably cutting up people in their basement or kidnapping little kids. The thing in this world, is you don't know people, and even when you think you do, and get surprised but what you find out, why does it surprise you? The world we live in now is a world where there are no more surprises. If in your gut, it doesn't feel right, then go with your gut.

Especially with drug addiction, if you think they do drugs, if miss sally may be at the end of the street corner, in her nice button-up shirt and plaid skirt, yes, miss sally may is probably doing drugs and is so good at it, you won't even know it. In the world we live in, we look at people, and just by the way they dress or what they do or who they are, we think they are not capable of things, but so much has come out in the media and our daily lives, that makes anything possible. Just don't think things are not possible anymore, because they are.

This is a disease of lying. If anything that I have learned from this uncontrollable drug of choice is you learn how to lie all the time and to not lie anymore is the hardest thing to reteach yourself.

What really gets scary, is are they that far in their addiction and injecting themselves? Because if that's the case, get tested! I mean it! When it gets that far along, luckily not with our case, there are dirty needles and people share and when you're high like how high you get from heroin or cocaine, yes, and agreeing is the only way! I'm sorry if that's your case and you're reading this, make the steps to protect yourself and others!

Like I've been saying this disease takes over the mind and controls that person and its people who care whether they live or die, who need to step up and help this disease. I'm writing this book for that very reason. I'm done being quiet! I want people to listen and stop doing the same thing! There's a very good chance all the people in this world know someone on drugs or that is prescribed narcotics.

This disease, opiate addiction, I want people to understand, it is, to me, like a pimp that breaks you down and makes you do things and controls you, it is like a cult leader of some religious camp getting into your mind and make you believe if you kill these people, you will have a special place in the grace of God or the devil, or if you listen to them, you will be saved once the world ends or die with the colony and drink the juice because the world is going to end. It is this type of reality a drug addict lives in and these drug dealers seek out these people, these weak individuals, and know by their demeanor, they can control you and will make damn sure you keep coming back for their drugs. My husband states you don't even know you're doing it anymore, it is a necessary need to keep going back for more, not just because you know you will go through withdrawals, but the nature is they have become your friends. He said to me, "I want drug addicts, if their reading this or the people around them to know, even if you think you trust the people you are buying from, trust and know, they don't even know what they are selling you, and it could be laced with something that will straight up kill you and stop all your organs in your body, and you will die. Do you make that risk? I know I did and I know it's the disease pulling me and keeping me going to those damn people, but you have to be strong and say no. You may not die on your next trip to the man, but you will eventually get the wrong batch and never know it."

IT IS NEVER TOO LATE TO GET HELP

My husband, like other people I have encountered regarding this disease of addiction, has said, "Try to get help, before it's too late, and remember it is never too late." It is never too late for anyone to fight this, and I know everyone has different situations, like you may be homeless, or may have no family or no one that cares for you, but there is someone that cares for you. You weren't homeless, to begin with, and you weren't friendless or familyless, to begin with, you probably had it all, and then one day, you were just down on your luck, and here comes someone who tells you it's OK or maybe it was just to relax you from a bad day, but there's hope and help.

I don't know if this disease will be one to ever be cured because there's still a need for pain medication for proper uses and I do not think we will ever be able to stop all the drug dealers and distribution within the country, but I want to try to at least raise awareness and maybe save one life and then another. I want to express, if you have no one else, you have us that believe in you and believe in this being a disease and want to help you. My husband, regrets more than anything, starting this drug thing and wishes every day, he could take it all back and is blessed to be here to try to redo what he can and remake those relationships he lost. He wants people to know, not only did he survive death and the disease kept pulling him back to just have him die again and barely make it out this last time, but all the people he hurt and all the people he lost. You will lose everyone, is that worth it? What is going on in your life that makes that worth it?

I've been with my husband, as you know 12 years, and I can't say he's stayed sober for more than three months. The disease keeps pulling him back in, keeps making the mind want and need, and he's never been strong enough to say no, even when knowing he will lose everything, not just me, or his family, as you found out, he was willing to die for mere dust.

You say to yourself, I've tried everything. Maybe you have but, we have gone through the 1st hospital visit from bleeding from the inside, which I found him passed out on the toilet in the bathroom, unconscious, which led to five days in the hospital, which led to me knowing the 1st time he was on drugs because he was withdrawing and mind you one month before we said I Do. This led us to the 1st detox program, then a pain management clinic to use Suboxone (an addictive narcotic to wean you off an addictive narcotic, yea doesn't make sense), then counseling, then nothing.

You have to remember, if the person doesn't want to get help for them then the counseling is pointless, it doesn't work. Even when that person is faced with therapy that doesn't allow you to come back if you test positive, you pray that is the answer.

STOP ENABLING

I still married him knowing the battle I would face. I felt I would be able to change the definition, the statistics, and change this new version of this man I've known, I am thinking, "I can do this!" But I was sadly wrong. From that point, five years ago, led to more fights, kicking him out a couple of times, broken doors and punched walls, and nothing but mental abuse, and then finally you start to live with it and accept it when you shouldn't! Accepting is enabling and for this disease, you cannot do that! You're going to end up where we did and me finding him breathless next to me. No heartbeat, no color. You don't want that! Prevent it because if you want to stay in that person's life and do nothing you better not cry when you find them dead because you were very well a part of it.

You never want to say what if? What if I talked to him more about his day? What if I really encouraged therapy or treatment of anything? What if I didn't let him take the car because I knew where he was going? What if I just stand by and do nothing when he's so lifeless sitting up on the couch that the dog can lick him for 20 minutes and he doesn't move? Don't ever say what if? Just do it! Trust me you are right! Your gut and yourself are telling you what's going on and as my friend said, "You're not that stupid?" And trust me, I felt that way. How could I just let things go and be that enabler when really all you're doing is hurting yourself and the person you love! Hopefully, in this next chapter, I can help you realize the signs I never did to try to help and address the issue before it's too late.

This disease will eventually shut your body down, maybe not now, tomorrow, next week, or maybe in a year, but this disease will eventually kill that person you love!

Chapter 4
Signs of Addict

When I talk about this topic, I have experienced or know from friends, regarding signs to look for, and maybe not all of this could apply or maybe some of it already does. Again, I just want to reach out and help people like myself that maybe are in the clouds and don't really understand or know what to look for. Some of this you may read and take it right away and say wow, that does apply, or maybe you disagree with it altogether. Just know all I am trying to do is help make your lives easier than mine and help save lives by trying to address the situation before it gets too far and there is just no saving that person from themselves.

    Here's a big eye-opener, if they are ready to party before the party even starts. I have to think back and actually every time we would host a party at our house, which we did plenty throughout the years, my husband would already look like he either smoked a blunt or drank about a six pack of beer. Hey, we were young, and buying our first house when I was like only 21 was like why not host the parties, since we were pretty much the only ones with a house or still not living with our parents. Parties always consist of weed and drinking but never seen anything wrong with that then, and it's been about to three years since we last hosted one. It's said, not because of the drinking and weed, but because I can't do that anymore because my husband is a recovering addict. I know we are in our 30s and should be toning it down, but my best parties were for New Year, Saint Pattys Day, and Notre Dame Football Games. You just can't enjoy those things with an addict anymore. It's like throwing it but not having him in his own house, that's not right. A lot changes for both of you. It sucks because I am an outgoing person and love hosting get-togethers, making all the food, my mom with her special punch, playing cards, beer pong, dancing to music, etc. I wish I would have seen the signs than with him, wondering why he looked so wasted but no one has even gotten there yet. Keep an eye out for this, it may be the right situation to find out if they are doing something that you can prevent.

Another sign is watching them just nod off completely. For example, I would know he was high when I would make dinner all night and then sit his plate in front of him and as he would move his fork into the pasta, let's say, he wouldn't even get it close to his mouth before falling asleep and the fork completely missing his mouth. Then you say, "Hey are you OK?" and his excuse is, "I am just tired, really long day. I'm OK, I love you poot," or it would be, "Stop it poot, why you keep yelling at me, I'm eating." He never would actually eat. It got so annoying that I finally would just take his plate and clean up because it just would piss me off to watch him just drift away and just act like he was wasted. At the time, we were drinking and having a few beers when we cooked, it was our thing then, so it was hard to tell if he was doing drugs or just really tired and a little buzzed.

That's a horrible excuse, he's doing drugs. If all else fails, always drug test. If they don't like that answer, then they're on drugs.

Right in the beginning of things, once we had our house, I would notice trips to the ATM he was making and drawing about 200 a week in cash. Now, before, I was allowing him to take out lunch money and gas money for his job, and from what I knew it was costing that much for the week. Sounds stupid, I know when I think back now, I was an idiot. Remember, stupid pullouts of large amounts of cash is up to no good, Unless he comes home with an awesome diamond ring, amazing vacation, or something else he wanted to surprise you with, he's doing drugs. It got to a point, where he was cashing his checks, and I had to call the bank and ask how much the check was for and they would tell me about 300 less than what was deposited. Luckily, when we first got together, he made me a part of his account at the bank so I could get this information, because let's face it, unless you're married, you really can't get anything about another person. If you're in a relationship, do what I did, start limiting his card to non-cash withdrawal, had all the money just being put in my account only, and limited what I gave him to just get him by and only credit card transactions no more withdrawing money and keeping all your receipts. Can it get that bad, yes it can and quick!

It's the most wonderful time of the year

Christmas, what a wonderful time of the year, and yes it was for us this last year. My husband was coming home every couple of days with tons of stuff he was buying from stores, just ridiculous stuff for his family and me because I usually shop for everyone, but he was doing some on his own. Now, how can a person with access to no money, buy tons of stuff? That should be a big red flag right there! There is no way he is buying that with money he earned, or maybe he did with selling the drugs he did. Some may think, well maybe he just opened a credit card, yea no, never think that. It may be the most wonderful time of the year, but it's not! Get real! At this time, I didn't know until after his cardiac arrest four times, that he was doing heroin and not only doing but selling it as well. Later did I find out, he was so deep into it, he was working four other cell phones to keep the supply and demand. When you learn all this, sometimes the truth hurts, and do with it what you may, but someone in the hard needs help or needs to be by himself.

So, the money he made off that is how we had a great Christmas last year and which also cost him his life. If big amounts of new things or new things start popping up around your house and he doesn't have any access to money and you know he's not getting money from his family or friends, guess what, its drug money. Be aware and make notice!

So keep an eye out, even for your families out their dealing with opiate addiction, this goes for you too. Watch what you give for Holidays, like what happened one year with us, his dad gave us a 100$ in an envelope card and my husband said I will hold onto it, well when he got home, it mysteriously vanished and he said he lost it to his dad. We could never find it, because it was never lost. He had an opportunity to gain free cash and took it and lied so he would have money to get his drugs. Then we decided to just give me the cash or gifts so I always knew where the cash was coming and going. Also, watch giving any cash whatsoever. Families listen up, heroin and pills are the easiest things to find and some can be very cheap especially heroin, so any little bit of money gives them an opportunity. Hopefully, this person in your lives has a significant other you can confide in, if not, you need to make that decision on your own. If this person in your life is working, they don't need gas money or lunch money or whatever money they have an excuse for and if they're not working, get them help because that's why they don't have a job.

Over the past couple of years, people I know have lost their jobs, because they are so far in they are stealing from people's houses. They don't have the means to say no, so when they go into your house for maintenance and happen to walk by your medicine cabinet, and let's say you're an older adult, you are going to have a good selection of pills they can either sell or use themselves. You say, why would they do this, when they could easily get caught and reported? Addicts don't care, in their minds, it's the next high and they could be out or need some at that time. Not saying all the people that come to your house you should be watching them, but unfortunately, I do, because I've been through it. Not only is it because they are working, but they do it for their own friends and family. I know of a friend that called me and said he had gotten home and saw my husband there and wondered what he was doing with his trunk open, and when he approached him, he immediately shut his trunk and said hey I was waiting for you but I have to go now. When he went into his basement, he had realized he had taken his video system with games and DVDs. When his friend called me, he said, "I am not going to report him, but he needs help and I never want to see him again. I am trying to stay clean and he isn't. He needs help, you need to get him to help soon." Now, I don't know if this is true but how can it be false, why would someone call who I know and say that out of nowhere? Never think someone from the outside is telling you false stories, more than likely they are true even if you don't want to believe them.

You start to notice things in your own house missing, to the point he even calls the police to try to say someone else did it and they can't find any other fingerprints other than his own and your own. First, it was his gun which he sold but said someone came in and took it. Then it was our speaker set, then our antique video game collection from Nintendo games to Sega in the original cases, and even our game systems, and when that was out, he started selling our tools and lawn equipment, saying people broke into our garage, and that very well could have been true but all the other stories you know make it seem impossible. Even in the car, he made it seem like someone broke in and took his speakers, when maybe so, but no windows were down or broken. Please be aware of these signs before all your stuff is gone! Do what you need to do to protect yourself and your hard-earned money! Some of this stuff, we can never get back.

People on drugs love not telling you where they are going and expect you to just understand and not question why? I think for most of our lives together have been a lie in some ways and not. My husband is a wonderful person, like any person, but he knew how to lie so well, I never asked twice, but we do trust people right off the bat until they do something dishonest and catch them in the lie and then that's when we hold them accountable. I don't think I will ever understand how someone who loves you, lies to you as well. I mean and lie to you in such a way, for many years, that you're to a point, is anything true? Is anything he tells me the truth or not?

We are in this chapter of our lives to discuss the signs of an addict, right? I can only go by my own experiences and try to share them in hope that people will find ways to discover them and stand up, and address them. So many people die from this epidemic that it's so sad it's over the start of a script given to you as a patient or a party you went to and was given something to "try." I think most people can relate to the symptoms of bloodshot or pin needle eyes. This sign is very present and can be noticed right away. Now in my case, my husband was actually prescribed, as you know, narcotics in the beginning, so this was normal for him. The point is, if you see this sign, it may be a way to discover something else is going on. My husband used to have these types of eyes all the time, even when he wasn't going to the doctors anymore and medication was not in the house you could see with the naked eye. Those eyes, even knowing this, should follow with signs of being unable to move fast or falling asleep in mid-conversation.

Other signs an addict will do, I hate to say it but love you. Yes, they will continue to say it, but how many people do that now, and say they love you just on automatic? People do this even without having a problem, but also, there is no affection that comes with the "I love you." Not just hugs or kisses, but sex. When someone is high on drugs, their desire to be with you is over. Sex to them is not anything they need any more or want anymore. Their libido is just not there. I could walk out naked or even try to urge him on, and nothing. I know I am not ugly or not attractive, but I look back on it now and then I thought I was. I was like "What's wrong with me?" You have this amazing sex drive with your significant other and then all of a sudden it's no more and it does get to you as a person and depression can happen and feelings of hopelessness and feeling bad about yourself. I want women/men to know that it's not you and you are beautiful and special and it's this awful addiction that takes over these people we love and they can't control it at some point and then it becomes, is it me? Remember it is never you!

My husband never really was a person who wanted to do things anyway, but that's a sign the person you love is being resistant or withdrawn from you when asked to do things. My husband would always say, "I'm too tired," or "I will be fine, you just go." He was always someone who loved to be home and there is nothing wrong with this, but for an addict, this is a sign of being distant. All these signs, I am describing, please remember it does not mean they are an addict, but it's a way to try to help indicate if there is a problem. Sometimes people are just lazy, let's be real here, so just keep your eyes open.

When I would be able to get him to go somewhere, I would also be on edge in the passenger side, as I remember, he would never let me drive and always wanted too, but when he would drive, he would close his eyes off and on and start to lean one way or another and then you're like what the hell is going on? I would sit there and tap him and say, "What are you doing and why are you driving off and on the road?" O, he would get so mad at me and just start yelling and cussing at me, and all I wanted to know is why? It's like them driving drunk, but with no alcohol. I cannot express enough how important it is to not get behind the wheel with someone like this, even if they yell and scream at you. I mean I had been with this man for years at this point, and I am like what changed? Again, you start blaming yourself and get nervous and anxious and think it's your fault. It is never your fault and you need to be strong and realize you're amazing and wonderful and you have to decide if you want to continue this relationship or get out when you can. My husband would always get angry and yell anytime he thought he was getting inquired on how he was acting or being accused of being on drugs. Be ready for this type of argument and the way someone can make you feel and if you are not a strong person, like me, going through this battle may not be right for you. I wasn't always strong, so don't let me lead you to believe that. It has taken years to be the person I am now and I am talking lots of nights of crying, being angry, "Why me?" and even thoughts of killing myself. Addiction affects everyone and everything around you. You just have to be strong or like I said before, or get out.

    Other ways I can say are a big red flag, at least in my life, is random people knocking on our door and my husband would be like, "Shhh, don't say anything and don't answer the door." Now, honestly, in this day and age, we don't answer to anyone we don't know or you shouldn't be anyways, but the way it was always said to not answer, was just weird and unusual. I can remember a couple of times, where this would happen, and after they would leave angry, and I mean sometimes they would be cussing and yelling at our door, my husband would all of sudden say he needs to go somewhere and ask me for money. I am not stupid, so I would say why and he would yell and argue with me because I wouldn't give him money no more because I knew something was going on at that point, but in the beginning, I'm like, when he would ask for money for fishing, or to go with the guys, or whatever the case is, I would give it to him because I was in the beginning stages of the lies with him and us. Later on, it made me nervous to be in my house, especially by myself for so many months, almost a damn year, due to his addiction. The reason I was scared was because at first, I really thought the two times our house got broken into literally was someone breaking into our house, so I got the security system.

I always wondered why my husband said it was a stupid investment after all the breaks ins we had but makes sense now because duh, it was stupid because he was the one doing them and making them seem to like it was someone. Even that being said, I was still nervous being home by myself, especially when all this addiction stuff came to light, because I didn't know who knew where we lived and did my husband owed people money and are people going to come to the house and collect. It was horrible once everything came out and all I could do was pray that no one would be coming to look for him. Of course, his phone was released to me, the only one I thought he had, and I went through his texts and Facebook messages and everything, and all I did was cry. I could not believe how much was going on behind my back and what was going on.

My husband's phone was only the beginning to understanding the true nature of his problem. As I am

"You Owe Me, I Will Find You"

looking through his phone and reading these messages because he was stupid and never deleted anything, but remember people are smarter than you think, and the messages I could read stated you owe me this, I will come to find you, and I know you have a pretty wife, and I know where you live. Now after reading those, I was scared. I had to shut his phone off and request a change of number, which helped, because after one day of him not responding to people on his phone, his phone kept ringing and blowing up. Little did I know, at the time, he was doing a lot more than just using, but actually being the dealer as well.

I should have known the issue was really bad when I saw this sign, and he was asking for help when I came home. I came home to a cut-up straw with a white powdery substance on the table in the living room with a small plastic baggie with skulls on it. Now, I don't know what drugs are supposed to be, because again, I was naive to only knowing cannabis was bad and somehow that was the only drug out there. When I found this stuff on the living room coffee table, my husband passed out, barely breathing, on the couch and he slept a long time that day. I did wake him up and say, what the hell is this? and he just looked at me and called me stupid and stated I didn't understand and it was nothing. He got up and then threw the stuff away and that was that. I think at some point I was just scared to say anything or maybe just didn't want to deal with it anymore. I am blessed in a way, I have the time to reflect on these times and say what I could have done differently, but some people don't get that option with their loved ones and the time is now to say something, don't wait for things to get to this point.

As I said before, little did I know how bad his problem really was until I searched his work truck? I had to go up into that hospital room and tell him hey your boss is coming to get the work truck today and he was all nervous and finally, all the drugs had withdrawn through his system and he was like, you can't have them pick up my truck because it needs to be cleaned out. I was like, why does it need to be cleaned out, and then another lie came into the light and here we go again to learn something new about my husband I did not know. I still don't even know why I helped him and should of just let them find all this stuff I found and hold him accountable, but of course, you are so in love and unfortunately, things at this point would also hold me accountable as well if it came down to the police and I am not saying this is the right thing to do, but I did go home and look into his work truck and see why he did not want them having the truck without it being cleaned out. Now, I did not find drugs, but everything that resembled drugs had been going on. I found things like lighters, burned tin foil, broken straws, and random pills. The one thing that really brought the light in was when I found his four other cell phones under his seat. I could not believe what I was looking at and then realized OMG, he is in this drug thing badly and he must be dealing as well. Then I realized how much I didn't know about what was all going on and how bad things were really.

I can remember the times he would ask for multiple stool softeners. I said to myself this makes no sense, a typical person cannot go through all this Miralax or Loperamide. Little did I know, he was because he was taking so many drugs, he could not have a bowel movement or a normal one. I do remember a time we had to go to the hospital, and this was one month before we were getting married, and he ended up in the hospital, admitted, due to him just shitting blood. That hospital visit, I think he was there for four days straight and coming off drugs then too, but he was released and at that time, I didn't even consider this was a drug issue, but it was. He was doing the hardcore then too and again, I just didn't even know it or chose to believe it.

A lot of us have pets, especially dogs, and my husband would also use this as an excuse to make a score. We didn't live in the best area, like you go two blocks over and it was the ghetto and then two blocks over, it was a nice area, and we were right in the middle. So, he would say I am going to take the dog for a walk and I would be like sure, that's great because of course, dogs love walks and him even showing interest in doing anything was great. I can tell you when people are on drugs, they literally have no energy to do anything. I mean we lived in that house for 13 years and he only started to care about doing things at all when he was finally off the drugs completely. So, I still thought it was odd that he would do this every now and then, but again, never thought it was because he had a problem. Sometimes, he would be gone for an hour and I am like, why in the world, but then I saw the dog happy so I am like awww.

This was something to the naked eye as an issue or problem. I should have known he had a problem when I tried to put a tracker app on his phone and yes, he agreed to it, because I knew something was up, but when he would leave, he would shut it off sometimes, and then when I would question him about it, it was a whole new story why did he need it and just yell at me and say why don't I trust him, etc. If you do run into this situation, try this option and see how they respond. This should have been a red flag, but it wasn't to me. Even when I would get phone calls from his family saying they saw him here or he was seen with this guy or even his friends pleading with me and telling me he has a problem, I still don't know why I didn't step up and make choices earlier. You have to listen to people, unfortunately, even when you feel deep down you should know this person and he said they're crazy and why do you listen to them. It's a control thing and again, you have to be strong and stand up for what needs to be done and let somebody know and try to help them.

Chapter 5
You're Not Alone

It may feel like you're alone, but you're not. It's hard to ask for help, I know, I never did and I wish I did sooner. The lonely nights of crying and feeling like you want to end your life because you do get to a point where it feels your whole world is crashing down and there's nothing you can do! Seek out! Get the help you need whether it's a best friend or a family member. I will tell you the best help you do is get yourself therapy because even if you don't think you're the issue, there are issues you need to be resolved before moving on or staying in the relationship you are in. I even had someone who has been through recovery tell me that too, "You need help whether you think you do or not" and they are right!

You have to remember when dealing with a loved one or someone you care about, they want to lie and make you feel alone and you're the one with the issue or maybe crazy. Addicts like to lie, it's in their nature to at this point, they want to hide their embarrassment and guilt and deal with their illness to themselves. They get so caught up in the lies that they feel this is the truth and the other people are lying. In an addict's life, from what I have witnessed personally, the lack of honesty is their way of life and the disease of the addiction keeps them in this twilight reality and there is no way out for them. My husband talks about his addiction now more than ever and I think it's a way to try to explain to me and people he loves to try to understand him and what it is like on the other side. He describes once you're in the game that far, you see no happy ending, you see no happiness, just this new reality of depression and sadness and no willingness to live. He believes that is why people die from this addiction because they have no reason to live and even if they do, they are so far in it, they don't see the good things right in front of them.

A lot of times, addicts feel like they cannot turn the switch off. My husband says it's like a little demon sitting on your shoulder and whispering into your ear, telling you to do all the bad things and even though he has an angel sitting on the other shoulder, that voice keeps getting more silent and more silent over time, that one day, that angel of a voice is no longer there and was just a memory, forgotten. He says you start to feel the cravings when you're not using and the chemical part of the brain just tells you, "I need, I need, I want, I want, give me, give me," and there's no way to shut it off by themselves so they continue to use to live a normal life in their eyes.

My husband, I feel, was never depressed or had issues he needed to use drugs for to cover up, but we don't always see what the naked eye can't see. Sometimes, the issues are right in front of us and we just can't see them. Addicts feel they need to continue with the drugs to cope and keep their life together, and it can be due to depression or an alternating life experience, but we must never ignore the signs like I did. Be brave and understand this person is going through something and the addiction is eating away at them and it doesn't matter what stage they are in, this is a progressive disease and the sooner you can address it, the better chance you have of saving their life.

Remember, like my husband, he was very isolated after a while, years with his addiction, and I didn't understand then why he was being that way, not wanting to go out, never wanting to do family events, just totally in his big recliner with no expression. Addicts will isolate themselves and continue to do so, because they live in life, a reality now where they do not see what they are doing is hurting the people around them. They start to deny, deny, deny, and make you feel like you have the problem and they hate you for even trying to state they have a problem and they need help. Remember to not let your guard down, and do not hold those tears back, continue to pursue to help them and give it everything you got, because it may make all the difference.

My husband has said to me the longer he was in the drug scene, the harder is it to get out and that makes sense. He says the reality he was living in was the new normal and he was to the stages of the disease to where he thought he had nothing to live for, even though he was coming home to a wife and a house and his dogs and just a normal life with love all around, the drugs made him feel like there was nothing to live for. The feeling of emptiness it supplies for the addict only gives them the one feeling, or should I say two feelings, urges and living.

The lying, I think for me, was the biggest slap in the face. Not all the almost death experiences, and the weird calls, texts, and knocks on the door, just plainly the lying. The man I knew and fell in love with was gone, and I would cry constantly at night and wonder why does he keep lying to me and why does he not love me the same way he did? You have to know this loved one to understand if they are lying. There are tons of suggestions to see if they are, but you should know when they are. My husband has this way of smiling or smirking when he is lying, and that would make it easier to know, but even if you know, will you do something about it? Don't feel scared and alone here, do the right thing, stand your ground, help them, they are crying out to you, trust me that is what it is. My husband even tells me to this day, that's what he was trying to do. Listen.

My husband was so far in the game, a lot of bad things came out of it by not stepping out earlier. None of these things that happen, remind yourself, are anyone's fault and maybe not even the addicts' fault, but with addicts, you can see they are having issues with opiate drugs by noticing how they react when you ask them the question of "Are you high right now?" Again, this is where the deny, deny, deny happens because it's not like when someone who drinks a lot, is like WHOA I am drunk or even when someone smokes weed and states, WHOA I am high, this is a different response, right? They just deny and that's odd because why don't they have the normal response to the high they are experiencing and that's because this is a different addiction. Remember this also, whatever they say, if they admit they are using, it's double or triple what they are coping up to and a good example of this is when my husband was in the hospital, and the doctor with his lab results in hand, explained to him, your lying because your lab results don't lie and you weren't just doing opiates, you were doing heroin, and again, he would just deny, deny, deny. Always remember, they will deny, but labs don't lie, tests don't lie, they lie.

You think with evidence like that, they would just be honest, but no. Then you may come across when the addiction gets real bad and they lose their job, but they may say, oh it's because of this or I was late too many times or it was over something stupid, but then later find out, it was due to complaints of people stating they had pills missing or stuff missing from their homes. It happens. They stop asking you for money because they are finding other ways to support their habits. Just because you won't give them money, trust me, that won't stop them. Keeping them from their bank accounts, won't stop them. Nothing will stop them, so they will refer to stealing in plain sight and selling your stuff, priceless stuff, to just get the fix. There are no ends or lengths, my husband stated, for an addict to get his fix. He or she will do whatever it takes to get what they need and it won't stop unless something helps change them.

You need help through the ups and downs and what I call the trickery. Trickery, for example, is when they say they love you and want to hold you and kiss you and then maybe even want to have sex with you, but then you get to realize it's only when they're high. Only when they are high do you get the affection you should have in a marriage or even a relationship. That is crazy and very disturbing, right? They learn tricks of the trade, per say, to live their everyday life and guide you through yours.

People all around the world are dealing with addiction. It doesn't even matter if you're rich or poor, it affects everyone the same way.

Even if you don't want to go see a therapist, reach out to the groups that are in the area you can just go and sit in meetings with and just listen. My friend told me about this. I haven't yet gone myself, but I feel it's a way to just hear and know that you are truly not alone. Just like me, you are probably using the excuse that you're too busy and can't fit it in the schedule or you're too broke to pay for the session. Look, therapy is never going to be cheap and in our case, we got lucky in a sense because we met our out of everything with the insurance so for the rest of this year it's free, but even so, you need it! Go to these free meetings you can sit in and listen. Make the time you need to feel good for yourself.

Maybe you just need a break? That is OK too. You need to never forget yourself through this whole ordeal. Whether you stay or you go with whoever this addiction is attached to, make your life yours again! Find a hobby or something you love to do and make the escape. I chose to dance. I've been teaching and dancing for a long time, and maybe I didn't even know it then, but it has been my escape. It my time to forget all that is going on and live again. Find that for yourself so you can make yourself a better you again. Loving life and yourself will help you face this battle of addiction if you choose to stay with it.

Maybe it's reading a book, or going on a vacation with your girls or guys, spending a Sunday dedicated only to you, or maybe it's even God. A lot of this time, I have been speaking with God. I have never been a true go to church every Sunday or reading the bible, but when this last time happened with my husband, I never prayed so much in my life. Most people would say he got lucky to be alive, I say God listened to my prayers. He was watching over this man and said, "It's not time for you yet!" or at least that was quoted by my husband from his out-of-body experiences he faced during his four codes. He said someone or something, as his body floated through the tunnel of light, said, "It's not your time, you need to go back." The fourth time he coded, he said he almost made it through the gates.

Religion is a touchy subject for a lot of people, but you don't need to be like I said the churchgoer to pray to God. It helped me through some of the times and when good results happened, I thanked him every day. At Least God or whoever you pray to in your religion is listening and not judging and sometimes that's the right person to talk too. It's someone you can clear your mind with and pray for guidance to get through.

I always ask myself, why do I feel this way? I mean I have everything, but the one thing I didn't have, was his love. I think about how we all, his family and friends, are going through the same things with him and no one is doing anything so this makes you feel like is it just me or does he have a problem? I almost want to scream at the top of my lungs, why is no one doing nothing, but I never spoke it. I never thought things would have gotten as bad as they did and wished to do things differently. The problem is there is no time machine to go back in time and that is only in the movies or your wildest dreams. Life is a one-time thing and what you do with it is your choice and yours alone.

Sometimes, listening to music helped me and touched me in ways I felt like I wasn't alone. I have always preferred 90s music above anything else because it was meant to touch your soul and make you feel. The music nowadays is just about clubbing and drinking and all kinds of stupid stuff, in my opinion. A song that related to me when I was going through the events after all this came out and opened was "Be a Man" by Aqua. When listening to this song, I can just feel all the hurt and the lies I was dealing with and it made me cry and be furious, but also helped me just get out what I was feeling. This part in the song, "I knew that I fought to keep our love strong. If you leave me now, you come running back for more, babe. And I hope for, and I wish for, And I pray, that the words from your mouth can, eventually make you a man." In a sense, I felt like I wanted him to tell me the truth and couldn't understand why he wasn't and why he wanted to toss it all away, and then I knew he would regret it later if he survived.

Then I would listen to our wedding song, "Marry Me" by Train and "Promise" by Jagged Edge and just cry and feel so hopeless by myself, but I needed to cry and feel that to make me stronger. Now I listen to, "We Belong Together" by Mariah Carey because honestly, we do belong together. I don't know many people who would have stayed with someone going through all that he did at the time and still be going strong today, but this song states it to me, "When you left I lost a part of me. It's still so hard to believe. Come back baby, please, 'cause we belong together. Who else am I gon' lean on when times get rough, who's gonna talk to me on the phone till the sun comes up, who's gonna take your place, there ain't nobody better, oh, baby, we belong together." And when it says, "When you left…" I referred to that when my husband almost died and then was gone out of my arms for weeks, months, while he was getting better. A lot of songs are an outlet, use it. Find those favorite ones that bring you together and then use them. Then find the ones that make you sad and just cry and get it out. Everything happens for a reason and there will be light at the end of the right tunnel.

We found ways to help my husband with going through his insurance to find him the treatment centers or the doctors, but if you don't have the means or insurance, try searching through Google and typing anything in like, "helplines for addiction" or "I need centers that treat my addiction." I honestly don't know what we ever did without Google, but this is a way to search the big, widespread internet and find ways to help that loved one. There's a way and sometimes it is just a click away. Rest assured, you will find somewhere or someone to help start the process and get that loved one and yourself back on the right track.

Now, since I have let my boundaries down and accepted the help I need, I now feel better about myself. I have help from his family, my family, our friends, therapy, and above all God. Trust me, you will feel better about anything you're facing once you give in and just let people help you. You will finally be able to take that deep breath and sleep at night knowing everyone is on the same page and will help not only the addict in your life but you as well.

"Family + Friends
+
Therapy + God
=
Healing Together "

Chapter 6
The World Around You and Real-Life Stories

As a family member told me, it's hard to even read or listen to because unlike my situation she has two amazing boys and she does that all by herself. As she says, "Years ago I wanted to help others with my experience." I lost hope. I tried so hard to save my family. I just gave up. Their dad would come and go and had stories for days. I finally cut him off. He stole everything from money to our souls. I had to give up on him. He's still lost…just not my problem. I only asked him to hold down a job and be stable and predictable. Haven't heard from him since. Sad sad sad. "I thank god every day I don't have children go through this with me. My dogs however suffer just the same, not getting fed and no water because he's too high to do it or passed out." Never go on walks, unless to get a fix, or play outside anymore because that's not a priority and when he rips me a new one regarding the ice cream and barkbox I get every month for them, I say at least I love and care for them. Again a person needs to love and care about themselves before they can for anyone else or anything.

I was speaking with a lady one day and she told me this story that wanted to be shared. "My daughter just came and took my car and drove off. I have been noticing signs and I have just been enabling her this whole time. I have been denying the reality right in front of me. Now she's gone with my car, with these men, and just doing drugs."

"She complained of nausea feelings, having bowel issues and she was having mood swings, I tried to get her to go to get counseling and I went with her to all her doctor appointments to figure out what was really going on with her, but then come to realize she was doing drugs again. I tell her she's a beautiful girl and you need to find men that will take you to dinner and treat you like the princess you are, and nothing sticks. Drugs overpower her and she starts to feel sick and needs to find her fix and then she's not my daughter anymore. She would tell me stories of how a 26-year-old OD on heroin and stuff like that to make me try to think she wasn't doing the drugs herself, but then these guys come around and the lies start happening and now she is out of the city with my vehicle killing herself and there's nothing I can do. Why didn't I see the signs earlier, and why can't I do anything to help her?"

One of my good friends, who we both love dearly, can relate to this issue and wanted to share her experiences with me. She had an amazing father, who loved and cared for her like any father would do but also had a problem. At that time, especially when we are young, we don't see everything for what it is. It's like watching a movie now that we did when we were kids and realizing, "O that's what they meant" or "OMG I didn't even catch that then." I think our parents try their best to make those things be unknown obviously, and another great example is when your parents tell you to go get a pop for them and really it's a can of beer. How would you know that then?

My friend told me about her father and these random calls he would get and speak in a coded way so it was like having a normal conversation. It got to a point for her, with all the strangers knocking on the doors and the dealers coming to the house, she found some other place to live for a while, even though leaving her younger brother back at home. She stated her father even admitted to her, as she remembers it, in the first grade, "I have a drug problem." Now, what is a little girl to do with that? What does anyone do with that?

When you're having someone tell you this story and you just feel for her. I felt and can relate to her and every one of these stories in some way or another and it's amazing and helpful. It really does help someone when you can get this information or thoughts off your mind and relate to someone. It's just so sad it's everywhere, just like a virus, and never going away. There needs to be some way to help these people, help us and make a difference. Control the unknown. Make it easier to seek help, make it easier to pay for help, just make it easier and if it was that easy, if it could be affordable and approved with or without insurance, we would be saving more lives today over this, I know it.

So here is another scenario, you end up in a relationship with someone for a long time, who you find out has the problem with drugs, but you're not like me and you just say the hell with it, I am not dealing with this and let him go. I mean there's nothing wrong with that, it's your choice if you want to deal with the addiction or not. Then, after a couple of months, you're out driving around, and you look around and see a car parked and you're like, that's my old boyfriend's car and then you notice him inside it, as you're driving by. Do you stop? Do you try to engage to say hello? In this case, it was like no, I will keep on driving, that part of my life is over. You get home, do normal routines, and then go to bed. The next morning, you're up and going, turn on the news and watch it with your daily coffee, and then there is a special update. "A body of a man was discovered in his car this morning and was pronounced dead on the scene." You stand there and it doesn't faze you at all, until the car that pops up on the screen and it is the person you once loved and cared for and you can't even catch your breath because you were just there yesterday. You were just there and could have stopped. Maybe it would have helped him from getting the final score or maybe just delayed the inevitable or maybe nothing said would have changed the outcome, but what if? I don't know this guilt myself, because my husband was saved, barely, both times in his life to death experiences, but I think I would be still asking myself what if, even now.

An addict can adapt and make things the way the person wants things in his world and mind game. They are so careful in the beginning and try to keep everything in order by lying their way around everything. They have to think up new excuses and continue to lie to never get caught, but eventually, they will mess up. It's hard to continue to lie and continue to keep up with the lies and the stories. I remember cleaning up the house one day and thought to myself, he keeps putting stuff in this cabinet area and I don't know what made me look up there after all the times I wondered about it, but I did. I found some blank prescription bottles and nothing stood out in my mind, and I thought well he must have been done taking his medications because, at this time, he was actually getting scripts from a doctor, who later got arrested and went to jail, but I thought OK, I'll just throw them out. So I did and never thought another thing about it. Weeks would go by and then I would check again and then that's when the conversation had to happen because I was continuing to find these blank bottles and none of it made any more sense. Remember asking an addict if this is there, they will deny, deny, deny, and more than likely start an argument because they have been caught. My husband was very good at lying and I thought I knew when he was lying like he would laugh and smile like I do when I get caught, but nope, he was so far in I think at that point and was so convincing, I believed him and just threw them away again.

Well, one day I was cleaning, I would say a month later and found these small baggies, like a stack, and I was like what are these and why do they have skulls on them? Of course, I confronted him yet again and nothing but, "I don't know what those are" and "Why are you blaming me for this?" and "I am so sick and tired of being blamed for everything." Little did I know, in any scenario I would check him with, I would get these same excuses and denials. I wasn't stupid, and I knew these were drug baggies, but it didn't matter how much I yelled or we argued, this little thing came popping up, in the laundry, the cabinet, etc. I finally was fed up with it and said you know what, I want you out of here. He started to cry and stated he didn't want us over and he had nowhere to go, well he did, but then he would have had to be honest with his family and he knew he couldn't do that, so he left. He was gone for two whole nights and claimed he slept in his car, to try to make me feel bad, and at that time, I didn't care, but we talked it out and he said I will never do it again, I love you and will make things right. Boy, was I stupid and let him back in my life and the house.

Finally to a breaking point and you have your mother-in-law come over just to yell at him outside the house to say, "What the hell are you doing? You're high right now! Look what you've done, look at your wife, she's exhausted and done! We are all done! You need help, ask, call, do something, if not, this happens again, you won't have to worry about your wife throwing all your shit out on the lawn, I will be here helping her do it! Then you can go to the drug dealers and sit there and get high all day and just kill yourself because we are done with your shit and having to worry about you!"

"Do You Stay or Do You Go?"

I would say I couldn't have said it better myself because face it, you're the one wondering if this time you wake up and never heard him stop breathing, is he going to wake up with you. You don't sleep or think about you anymore because you're wondering where he is or what he's doing? It's real-life people, that's what it is! It's a loveless relationship you start to have with this person because you can't trust a single thing that comes out of their mouth let alone think it's going to get better. You have to decide if this is the right thing for you knowing they will always be an addicted. Like a friend of mine said, "Like I said last night, it's ultimately your decision on what you do and nothing needs to be decided overnight. It's a process. I do hope you really know that you have given it your absolute best. If you ever want to throw in the towel, don't feel like you didn't try everything. There will always be something else that will keep you there and keep on trying. For example, if this counseling doesn't work, it will be back to rehab and then you may feel obligated to stay for that, and then if that doesn't work there will be something else. There will always be something else, but you have already given enough and shouldn't feel bad about leaving if that is what you decide girl." She's right, you and only you can make this decision, and doing what's right will never be easy. It's like that song, "Do I stay or do I go?" That's exactly how hard it is to make that decision!

Finally, having that person show you the houses of the drug dealers and places he goes, and calling and reporting to your local PD. You're trying to save the lives of other people, even though there will always be another drug dealer that will come along, another person to sell another person drugs, but at least you're stepping up and making the right decision and trying to end the battle one piece at a time.

Chapter 7
What's the Next Step?

When you think about what the next step is and you think you have it all together and everything is going as planned, and then you get a knock on your door on Labor Day and it's your husband's boss and you're thinking for one who knocks anymore and two why is his boss here? You answer the door and say, "How can I help you?" And before you can say that, he says, "We found your husband unconscious in his work truck and he is at the hospital right now." My heart literally stops and I start to shake and as I try to keep it together, he comes in and says let me give you my number so you can call me and I am in such frantic mood that he has to put his number in because I can't stop shaking and thinking is this it? I am finally going to have to claim my husband's body.

I quickly grab my stuff and leave trash and food out and around and just leave my dogs the way they are and turn on the alarm and I am out the door. As I am driving, I call the hospital and ask for my husband and the nurse gets on the phone, and I scream, "Is he alive?" and the nurse says, "I can't answer that over the phone…" And I said, "All I want to know is he alive?" screaming to the top of my lungs and crying so loud I don't even think I understood what I was saying and the nurse says, "He is alive, he is in critical care, and try to get here as safely and as soon as possible." I hang up the phone and just start crying so hard, it's hard to even drive, and keep yelling out loud, "Don't you leave me today, don't you leave your poot." "There is not a world without my moot in it." "Don't you do this to me." As I am shaking, driving, and crying, I start to think did I say I love you last night, yes I did, did we say I love you before he left for work this morning, yes we did, and he even said I will see you later poot. I kept thinking to myself if he was just going to kill himself this time, why would he say all that?

Earlier that day, about 11:48 am, I re-posted on Facebook one of my favorite pictures from our wedding, and I quote, "If I could think of anyone I would rather spend the rest of my life with...that person is you! Even though the craziest year, we've had yet...you, my one and only moo! I love you!" That was on the day he attempted to kill himself as I described and he was unconscious at this moment and almost dead when I thought about him and posted this quote with a picture of one of the happiest times in our lives. With addiction, and especially opiate addiction, you never know what's going to happen next, you try and try and hope for the best to try to beat this drug, and it keeps creeping its way back up to you and people around you and I almost lost hope into finding a way to keep my husband in my life and the lives of others like his family and friends.

"Treatment is ONLY the beginning"

I wanted to end this book with this chapter and to let you know that this life you have with an addict, and in my case, a very disabled person now, can be wonderful, but also very challenging depending if they actually survive this reality. Daily, I am reminded how thankful all our family and friends are that I have made my husband get through this and even though he has his mental conditions and disabilities from his stroke and heart failure, they are just happy to see him healthy again alive. It's an uphill battle every day, let me tell you, and not everyone, I am sure I have said this a lot, but it is a trying day every day and you don't know who you are going to get, it's like Dr. Jekyll and Mr. Hyde. It's a new love you have for this person, it's a new world and a whole new life you are building with this person now. I did want to include things we went through to get him the help he needed and things that worked for me to get through this with him. There is no guarantee in any of this and whether or not this will help but, I wanted tools to be available for my readers to try because I never knew what step to take and what the next step should be, especially after we finally had him stable and he was still alive. That's the first battle, getting him stable and then moving forward with steps to treatment.

One of the things I started with my husband, even before his hospital visits and times with death, was a tracking app. I can tell you this will be difficult because they obviously do not want you to know anything and catch them, but if you can, do it to their phone when you know they won't see you doing it. I know that is tricky and I had to wait till he was asleep, but I did put in a spot on his phone I knew he would never see it, and later, this app ended up saving his life on the day they found him on Labor Day unresponsive. Now, let's say they catch you and find out you have done it, you want to deny it because you don't want the argument, but how I put it to him was, in case something ever did happen to you, wouldn't you want me to help find you?

There are two scenarios that could happen and one being, he or she gets mad at the fact you have been tracking them and they delete, but you can always put it back on so let them vent and be done. In another scenario, he or she agrees with you and it almost makes you think, maybe they want to get caught and they are crying out for help, but you want to know this for sure. Either way, I would try to keep this app active and hope it will help to find out things, but remember accusing them and fighting with them, in the beginning, will only get you denials and lies, and I would suggest to confined in a friend to help, maybe a close friend to him, or family member so that there is help together when talking to him or her.

Now, you have passed the phase with the app and trying to keep him or her on a leash, well and that seems to be working in a sense, but I found random drug tests, for me, was the next step. I would randomly drug test him and watch him pee. Now, I know how this may sound, but I cared so much about him, I wanted him to get caught in a sense to see, you need help. Well, even when the results showed up positive, there was still denial. I had our best friend aware of what was going on at that time, and she even tried to explain to him these tests are legit and you're testing positive and need to stop this shit. Well, I think this may help, but this won't solve your addicts' problem. It may help to gather needed "evidence" per say to help the bigger picture and get him to admit finally get help.

Through this whole battle of addiction, I am sure you're asking yourself, can you trust this person again? That is such a hard question and I don't think there is a right answer. I asked myself in the beginning, once he was back at home with me, can I trust him? Well, I can say I trust him a little more every day. What I mean is, by him doing things and confirming things they are true, we can see together the honesty. I mean he would let the tracking app always be alert and on, and that made me trust him a little bit, then he made his phone available to me and say he's keeping on the honest track, and that helped me a little more. I think the topping of the cake for me was when he had picked up a phone call and said I am not doing it anymore and I don't want to talk or see you anymore. Then we ended up blocking people on his phone and they said I want to get a new number, and we did that too. I believe if they show they want to change, you trust them a little bit more every time. We are about three years since the last time he was in the hospital and did drugs, and I can tell you I still have issues with trusting him, but we grow stronger every day together.

You may never trust that person again and then maybe it's time to step away, but that's a choice everyone needs to make on their own. Again, there is no right or wrong way in this addiction. You have to think of yourself and the people around you and can you keep this person in your life. I can't imagine having children with him and deciding that factor, but those are the factors that may be in your life and what's safe and right for them. I don't know that answer, but there's always a way to try to help them.

Treatment is a way to try to help them. Unfortunately, in the society we live in, sometimes treatment isn't covered by our health insurance. Now, don't quote me on this, but I have found out that commercial insurance is very picky on how they cover things, to the extent of counseling versus therapy for instance. It's the same thing and can be coded the same way, yet the insurance will say one or the other is not covered. Now, if you have Medicaid, or Medicare, I believe these services are covered regardless. Medicare and Medicaid seem to cover everything to an extent, like a percentage, but with commercial insurance, you better make damn sure it does or you will be stuck with a huge bill, in the end, I know because I am dealing with that right now.

I still think now, why the hell does it cost so much to get the treatment you need to survive? I mean it's thousands of dollars like $30,000 or more for one month of treatment. Basically, if you don't have insurance, you're shit out of luck, because who in this world has money like that hanging around, no one. Can anyone afford treatment costs like that? It's almost like it is just cheaper to just die, right?

I can tell you by the experience of doing detox centers to actually inpatient help, it was an uphill battle to get these things covered by insurance. Now, the detox center was covered by insurance. It usually consists of a week or two and then they are released and set up with outpatient services and a doctor who can write for Suboxone or some kind of medication to help with the addiction. We tried this way, back in 2015, if I remember correctly, to try to get him to help then, and this was two years before he almost successfully died, and let me tell you something, I feel like it was a joke.

You pick up the sober person from the facility and routine they have had for only one week or 2, and then you are given the doctor's name who can write the medication to help try to keep them sober and then the place to make sure they get their counseling. If these people do not have a good support system or even if they do, they will go right back to it. I mean you can try to keep eyes on them and have people check on them, but ultimately, they will be left alone and on their own thinking of things and ways to get their next score. You have to remember, not all addicts are in that bad and you may be able to catch it early enough and then this type of help will work and keep them on the straight and narrow, but in my case, this worked on him being sober for I think only a month after he was released.

Now, you're thinking well I am going to get a bill for these services, and even if you had insurance, it still will only cover so much. I ended up getting a $600 bill I think and then, I was the only one working at the time and had a mortgage and all kinds of bills so any added expense for something like this will make you mad and I know because I was and let's not even get started on Suboxone at that time and how much that cost. This medication was new to the market at this time and it was only coming in the strips and insurance wasn't covering it at this time. The cost for one month was $550 and you have no choice but to get it because they need to be stable and be on it. Now, luckily, the medication comes in generic and is covered by all insurances, especially Medicare and Medicaid as well, so need to worry about that per say, but then, it was so impossible to keep up with everything, bill wise, due to these unnecessary expenses for something, at that time, I did not understand. Things were definitely more difficult then, but things still are difficult and not cost-efficient for addicts to get the help they need to survive.

Even the doctor they end up setting up to treat you and give you your medication was a big fat joke. He would literally come into the room to see my husband and just sign off a script and hand it to him and say see you next week, because starting out, they need to see you every week and do urine screens. We'll be ready for this one, and by the way, there was only one doctor in any mile radius writing these medications, and my husband had a bad screen and that's because he had a slip up. OK, this can happen. Sometimes, there are slip-ups in the recovery, but these doctors won't take it lightly, and guess what? They dismissed him on the spot. Even after we had his therapist write the doctor a letter, he still wouldn't treat him. So, now you have an addict, who will eventually detox basically at home from the Suboxone, and now will need to fend for himself. What kind of treatment is that?

Well, as you know, we tried this treatment in 2015 and noted in this book, he had his heart failure due to drugs in 2017 so, obviously, this did not work. Addiction is tricky, it's a way of life that is just sometimes not even noticeable with the naked eye. We went on those next two years as normal and I think he was moving in the right direction, back to work, and doing things that were normal at that time, I was just going with the flow. After his heart failure in March 2017, we proceeded, as a family united, to proceed with finding him inpatient care. Not this was not easy, because again, insurances are not covering these services at this time, so check with your insurance on the benefits and you do not have insurance, check with these facilities, because they do offer grants and work-related programs to help pay your way.

We ended up finding a facility for him that would take, even with his recent device implant due to his heart failure and that had to be monitored due to it being implanted, but the place was almost three hours away. It was so hard to make that decision, because I just got him back, and then to let him go again so far away, but it was necessary to get him away from his surroundings and try to get him the help he needed.

He was in the facility, I think for one month, and then I got a call, our insurance will not cover the services he has been getting there. The way I know they offer grants at these facilities or work-related payment programs is because that is what he needed to do to pay for his services and we never saw a bill from them, which was a blessing because again, services are close to $30,000 for just a month. He did have to write a letter and submit for the grant, but he also helped clean the facility to help pay his way.

No one can really say this will help overcome their battles with addiction, but it is something to try. I remember visiting my husband every weekend, every weekend I would drive three hours there and three hours back to see him and give him encouragement to continue his way to better him. You only get two hours to visit with them and it's hard to leave, but I could tell he was getting healthier and things were moving in the right direction, so it was good, but still hard to leave him. I used to hate the phone calls because they would only allow a nine minute conversation literally, and the phone would hang up at exactly nine minutes. This was really hard when it came to me finding out our dog, Sugar, who was 11 at the time, had lung cancer. Man, was that a bad day. This dog was my husband's best friend in the whole world and his life. Now, how do you try to explain this in a nine minute only conversation? I debated the whole day, do I tell him when he is so far away, because we didn't know if she would live another day or a month or a year, it was just too hard to tell and Cancer had spread so much throughout her body already. See, this is what I am talking about, these decisions, these things that can happen, big major things, and you have to be in treatment and can't leave and these are things that happen.

I did end up telling him that night because if she died and he was not there, he would have been so devastated and hateful maybe toward me for not saying anything at all. Well, he was able to come home three weeks later, but not completely home. Unfortunately, I was a very busy person, not only was I working as a medical assistant in a doctor's office five days a week, but I also was a competitive dance teacher and taught classes three times a week, so I was never home really and in the early days of treatment, it's a good idea to have them being supervised all day to help not only with their addiction but, in my husband's case, his cardiac care. So, we did agree on him staying with his mom for another month or two and letting him come home on the weekends to spend time with me and our two dogs, which was good because we didn't know how long Sugar would stay around. Gosh, I have pictures from when he would be home with them on the weekends, and just the love he was finally giving them and me, felt so good, but in my life and I still live by this, I am always waiting for the other shoe to fall.

This is where I don't know if this system of treatment really helps addicts, because eventually, he was able to come home with me and he was able to go back to work that July 2017. I could see a big change in him and he kept in contact we would discuss things again and feelings were back and love was there again and it finally felt like things were back to normal. I remember when Labor Day came, that year, and as you know the knock on my door happened and yet again, we were back in the hospital and this time I didn't think we were going to make it. This is where I do not know if after paying all this money and doing all these things to help prevent the addiction from continuing to happen and it still happens, is it worth it? To even try?

I can see at this point, you would be just tired, just completely and overly exhausted and tired of just trying to make things be away, they just seem they wouldn't be. Hell, I didn't even know if he was going to be able to walk again or talk again, let alone survive this blow to him. I am going to say this, sometimes it is not the fault of the system and it may be the fault of the individual and the sickness that wraps their brains every day. I feel and have seen that sometimes a person needs to go through everything he has to realize life is worth it and that's if they survive all that to make it this far. That is why, and it's a touchy subject and not something at 30 years old I would think I would need to do, but get POA, power of attorney, paperwork done, and a will completed, especially when you have two families like his and everyone thinks they know best. Not everyone is lucky as we are and have a friend, who is a lawyer, who could come up that day and get this paperwork together and notarized. We are very blessed and lucky, but it is something to do because you want yourself protected and your family, but also want his final wishes to be honored how he would want them.

This friend of ours also came in to help us get his treatment documents to be released to us as well. Now, tell me this, how can someone afford to get something notarized if they're a drug addict and need their records. You need to get a notarized release to retrieve any mental health records. Well, I was pissed about this that is for sure, especially when the doctor they referred him to, to continue treatment, would not see him until these records were reviewed. Now, where does that system fail for any other addict trying to get these? They don't even have enough money to eat or drink or sleep somewhere, and you expect them to pay someone to get something notarized just for a doctor to review and may or may not take you on as a patient? What kind of messed-up crap is that? I feel this is where the system fails people in the treatment world. I feel they think everyone is a rock star or celebrity and has money coming out of their ass, well they don't and their needs to be a system in place to help people who really want to be helped and make it affordable to them.

One thing is to not give up! Now that Google is available, try to just search for addiction clinics or group therapy facilities to reach out and get help. I know my family suggests churches and they do offer sessions that are free for people and families to attend to help with addictions. Try the back of their insurance card and find out anything and everything that will be covered. Reach out to the family doctor they are seeing and see what options they can provide. Reach out period. There are tons of ways and options for people and all you need is to look if you don't have the money or support to reach out to on your own, go to your local church or homeless shelter and say you need help. I refused to give up on my husband and I refused this disease to take him and even through all the financial battles, all the fights, all the almost-death experiences, we are now living our best life.

PLEASE pick up your phone and call 1-800-662-HELP

A great number and outlet to try is the national helpline SAMHSA and their phone number is 1-800-662-HELP or you can also try this 24/7 hotline United Recovery Project and their phone is 1-888-634-0973. As well as if you Google, "Help centers for drug addicts or ways to help a drug addict to recovery," will give you other options as well. There are ways and tools to help these people and I am hoping there are more people out there like me, who will step up and at least try to save these people. We are facing this epidemic as a whole and the deaths keep climbing every year, and currently there are more than 46,000 people a year dying from this. That is about 3,800 people a month, about 126 people a day, and about five people an hour die from this disease. Five people an hour, can you believe that? It is right up there to pneumonia and flu deaths. Sometimes you cannot help getting the flu or pneumonia, but there is something you can do about addiction.

Something needs to happen and I want to make a difference in these numbers. No one needs to die, no family has to go through what we did, but if we knew then what we know now, maybe we could have made a difference and I want to do that now. No more death. Let's see the number of survivors grow and become more than the deaths in this country and others.

Then you hope one day, things will move in the right direction, and you will see the positive turn around and the hope of helping actually comes into light. I hope one-day I and my husband will actually be intimate and it feels like it finally means something to the both of you. The way he plays his nose thing with you like just rubbing our noses together, stupid little things, you just know when he says, "I love you," you just know he means it then. It's so hard to explain, but it's a feeling that overcomes the lies and the missing trust and then you just know he's finally feeling good about himself and starting to love himself again, so then he tells you he loves you and you actually get the sense of relief. The sense of finally feeling the deep expression of love from your significant other.

I hope that one day he will be that person I love and the person I dreamed of and the prince that watched the princess walk down the walkway in the beautiful forest and gave me that amazing look of wanting to spend the rest of his life with me.

I think back to even when we started, and I can't even imagine someone as kind and caring and not always thoughtful but this childish boy that I'd loved and meant that first night and how he just cared for me when he didn't even know me, and to think he could get mixed up and to think we would even be here at this moment in our lives. All I can hope and really is hope is that I do my part and he does his, and we try to make it through this awful stage in our lives.

It's almost like it never happened! Even though I know he died, and he came back, and even though he did it again and now has suffered a severe stroke, which has partially paralyzed him in Vision and severe damage to his brain, which has led to possible seizures, Even though he walks and talks and still jokes, still see these memories and feelings, these things in him, that have not have changed. You almost wonder if it is really enough, if this second, third, even fifth chance at life is going to keep him from being an addict, and you always hope you're not wasting your breath or time or moments in life, to take care of someone who, with no help or support or counseling, will do it again. What will be your choice?

You have to say to yourself, is this what I want to do? There is no right or wrong answer. Love is so hard for any to explain, love is something that keeps pulling me back to him. I can't imagine spending my life with anyone else, even after it all, I still cannot imagine my life without him. All I want to do is take care of him and make a better life for him and myself. You have to remember your body, your soul, yourself can only take on so much, and even as much as you love a person, and you do everything in your power to keep them strong and healthy, especially in this case with the awful influences, drugs, and society itself, this epidemic reaches beyond that! It reaches people somehow by just walking down the street, just passing someone, or by someone's house, triggers happen every day and there is just no way you, yourself can prevent it! You try, try, try, and family try, try, try!

My husband is not even living with me because he needs someone with him all the time. He can't have his phone, because of wanting to call his dealer or supplier, and he lost his vision, so he can't even drive, which most people would say is a good thing, but is that enough? Eventually, life will go back to normal, eventually, he will have to go back to being an adult and have to do things himself, even if he can't drive, does that really keep him from the drugs?

You can't keep them from that, you can only try to keep them from that. It's an inevitable thing that only he can control and he has to find his way. Like I said, I thought it would be a one way street, a one way smooth path to the rest of our lives, and now it's this curvy, sliding down the hill, road, that I am not sure if we will ever make it back up the road again. I am ready to take the risk, because I know he loves me, deep down, and I love him. Those times we do spend together, remind me of those reasons I love him. People wonder why I stick with him even after everything, especially the nights of crying, worried, being upset, mad and angry. I still for some reason can't see myself without him by my side. I say to myself, Life will work itself out, Life is a tricky ninja, as I would put it, and Love is a tremendously tricky ninja! You will have your ups and downs and curvy paths, but if you truly love someone, you truly care for someone, you will be their side until you can't be no more. Can true love conquer all?

As I said before and will end this story on this note, You need to remember you! You need to tell the person that is going through this addiction, "Never be a prisoner of your past. It was just a lesson and not a life sentence." Be strong and willing to make the right decision! Life sucks and no one says anything about ever being easy. Whether it's your father or mother, husband or wife, brother or sister, child, or even your best friend, sometimes you have to stop being the enabler and cut ties! Hold your ground! You're stronger than you think you are! Believe me, after 16 years, I finally have done it! Hold my own and believe in myself! Whatever you decide, whether to keep that person in your life or dismiss them, like one of my friends said, "So who cares if you love an addict, do you!" Just remember to not enable them! Remember even through all the mess, the fights, the financials, the emotional scars, everything, just remember there's light at the end of the tunnel.

Sobriety is the key to Happiness and Full Life

Our story is still going strong, we are three years in sobriety, and I say "we" because you will be doing this together and not by yourself. You need the support system to help make the reality happen and I support him every day. We had sold the house we had been living in for 13 years, we sold all of our stuff, packed a van, and moved to Florida. We wanted a fresh start and yes, we moved halfway across the country to do so and I am not saying that's a solution, but for us it was. He is getting different treatments down here and is doing so much better and staying healthy. This new adventure we have made for ourselves has helped him be the best person he can be, and even with his disabilities and lifelong changes to himself, we have found a way to be happy again. We even got another dog, a service/emotional support dog for him and that is also helping his recovery.

My husband and I find ways to pass all the bad and look forward to all the good we will be able to still do together and this is a way for us to do something good and maybe help somebody else in a situation we have gone through. My husband still thinks he may not live long and worries about the what if, and it's so hard to see him wondering how much longer he will be on this earth, and I tell him every time, "God did not save your life, once, but twice, to just take you away from me again so soon. God is watching over you every day, watching over us, and as long as you stay clean and true to yourself, God will keep you with me and we will live long lives and grow old together. You still have plenty of life to live with me and I wouldn't change a thing." He always looks at me after I tell him this with such a calming, sincere look, and says to me, "Your right, I know, I still just worry about it because I never want to leave you again." Those words and this conversation just remind me of why I stuck around and love this man.

In the words of an addict, "Addiction is a forever battle and it will never end for the rest of your life. You will be tempted and you will have urges, but you will need to find it in yourself to make the right decision and decide what is important to you. Sometimes, those things they teach you in treatment do help and come into play, but ultimately, it's your life and your decision. My life took me down some dark paths, dark hallways I felt was the right way at the time and then I found God because I saw the tunnel of light and had to make that choice. No one, especially being as young as I was, should ever have to go down the tunnel and actually make it to the golden gates that should never happen. I am just blessed to have an amazing wife who has stuck by my side. With her and the help of family and God, I have found my way. It has been hard and it's a battle every day, especially with my brain condition I have now and the uncontrollable bursts of sadness and crying and other things, I chose life and say no to drugs. Drugs kill and have even taken close friends of mine away as well. I want to stay sober for myself and you need to get there as an individual to make things real. My life has been affected and I have lost out on a lot of things being addicted to drugs over the past 10 years and it will never be worth it. It will never be what you think it will be. Life is more important to me now, and I wish I would have seen that long ago and maybe made a better choice and taken treatment seriously and not been left with all these health conditions and disabilities that keep me from living a full life. Please consider your life and treatment for yourself because there is a better light at the end of the hallway and not finding the light at the end of a tunnel."

The main goal is maintaining sobriety and saving their life because deep down you love and care for them but you can only do so much! Treatment and sobriety are in the eye of the beholder and they have to do it for them and no one else!

My husband and I wanted to end this book with a statement from him and he wants everyone to know, it will never be too late to want to change yourself and don't make it too late and end up at the pearly gates and having to make the choice, do it now, so you can live life and have all these wonderful experiences because you get one life and that is it. Our journey didn't end, but it could have so many times, and he wants people to know he is so blessed to be living the life we are now and there is light at the end of the rainbow, we call it, there is wonderful things still to be learned and done with this precious life we are all blessed with. Try to make a difference and try to do what you can, every life is important, just like every child that is born into this world, it can be new and amazing again. Destroy drug addiction, like he says, and keep moving forward with sobriety. If he can do it, with no resources at all, everyone can do it.